RESEARCH-INFORMED
TEACHING
WHAT IT LOOKS LIKE IN THE CLASSROOM

EDITED BY **DR. IAN KELLEHER,**
GLENN WHITMAN & **RICHARD COCO**

FROM HODDER EDUCATION

Although every effort has been made to ensure that website addresses are correct at time of going to press, Hodder Education cannot be held responsible for the content of any website mentioned in this book. It is sometimes possible to find a relocated web page by typing in the address of the home page for a website in the URL window of your browser.

Hachette UK's policy is to use papers that are natural, renewable and recyclable products and made from wood grown in well-managed forests and other controlled sources. The logging and manufacturing processes are expected to conform to the environmental regulations of the country of origin.

Orders: please contact Hachette UK Distribution, Hely Hutchinson Centre, Milton Road, Didcot, Oxfordshire, OX11 7HH. Telephone: +44 (0)1235 827827. Email education@hachette.co.uk. Lines are open from 9 a.m. to 5 p.m., Monday to Friday.

ISBN: 9781036003296

© Dr. Ian Kelleher, Glenn Whitman & Richard Coco 2024

First published in 2024 by
John Catt from Hodder Education,
An Hachette UK Company
15 Riduna Park, Station Road,
Melton, Woodbridge IP12 1QT
Telephone: +44 (0)1394 389850
www.johncatt.com

A catalogue record for this title is available from the British Library

MIX
Paper | Supporting
responsible forestry
FSC™ C104740
FSC
www.fsc.org

Contents

Foreword

This is a collection of stories of what teaching and learning can look like when it is informed by research. We deliberately use the term "story" as our teacher-authors have shared snapshots from their journeys using research to transform their work with students each day. What sets each of these stories apart is the deep intentionality—how each teacher uses evidence from research, mixed with their professional wisdom and subject knowledge, in myriad ways to design everyday experiences. They are a fascinating insight into the depth of thinking that goes behind what, on the surface, might look like a simple learning activity. Like true maestros in any field, masters of their craft make the exceedingly complex look effortlessly easy.

The stories are written by early, mid-, and late-career teachers and school leaders. They span every age and every discipline. They show that wherever you may be in your professional pathway, there are great educators like you who are using evidence to elevate their daily practice and work with every student. This collection also includes stories from nine students and one parent to give insight into what happens when a whole school decides to use evidence to inform its practice. They begin to tell a story of impact.

We began collecting stories for *Research-Informed Teaching: What It Looks Like in the Classroom* to highlight a critically important point: research and researchers cannot tell teachers exactly what to do in their unique classes with their unique community of students. One of the great opportunities and challenges of becoming a research-informed school, district, or teacher is that "making it work in my context" is a most vital step in the translation of research to practice. We use the word "informed" intentionally because it involves teachers laying the promising principles from research alongside a host of other factors: their professional wisdom, their subject knowledge, their knowledge of their students and their community—and their own particular teacher secret sauce. I can read a hundred academic papers on retrieval practice, for example, but what does it look like this Tuesday afternoon in my math class? This is the essence of the stories in this compilation.

There is a growing body of academic research that could have a tremendous positive impact on students' academic success, well-being, and whole school experience—you will see a lot of it in the footnotes to each article in this book. Dr. David Daniel, one of our mentors on our professional journeys, reminds us that all research that we are considering is only "promising principles" until it is tried out in your context with your students, and you have gauged what the impact is and what the side effects might be. So this is our challenge to you: find one chapter here that resonates with you, read some of the footnoted articles, figure out what it could look like with your students, try it out, see what happens, and then share your story. The stories in this collection reflect one school's approach, with its teachers, students, parents, families, and broader community, to becoming research-informed. But the landscape of education desperately needs more real-world examples. So as well as being a model, we hope we inspire you to join us on this journey.

We know from the Center for Transformative Teaching & Learning's (CTTL) own research, through its freely available Neuroeducation Confidence Diagnostic, that there is a huge gap in teachers' knowledge about how the brain learns best, and their confidence in translating this into learning experiences for their students. This is not surprising since the science of teaching and learning is rarely a required part of undergraduate and graduate school education programs or other pathways to professional certification and entrance into the teaching profession. These stories can be a potential catalyst for such professional growth and a school's continuous professional development. Amid the stories in this volume are the perspectives of students who validate how having research-informed teachers has transformed their academic, social, and emotional development, as well as their mindsets for learning. Including the student voice in this publication is critical to us.

We hope that these stories provide a further catalyst for your continued professional growth.

As you move into reading this book, we want to let you know that while it may seem like we wrote it for you—the teacher, school leader, or policymaker—in fact we wrote it for your students. Every age, every subject, every type of school, every district, every program, every student, neurotypical and neurodivergent—everyone at all times benefits from a teacher who is on a professional growth pathway to being an even better teacher. What the stories in this publication show are glimpses of what is possible when teachers prioritize getting to know their students and building strong positive relationships—and then layer on top of this a whole host of other daily practices that align with how the brain learns best. It is a glimpse into what schools could be—a future where every student at every age had a expert teacher in every class, every day. What could be possible then?

In 1997, John Bruer wrote *Education and the Brain: A Bridge Too Far.* We hope we have laid this attitude to rest by helping you imagine a world where everyday practice in schools is informed by research as a matter of course. There is a long way still to go, but we hope that *Research-Informed Teaching* serves as a waymarker for how far we have come.

Acknowledgments

Since 2012, St. Andrew's has been sharing stories of research-informed education in its publication, *Think Differently and Deeply*. The first four volumes contain ninety-five stories. It was hard to choose just thirty for this book, which is why there are forty-eight. The authors whose talent, passion, and wisdom we are sharing are the real stars of the show, so they deserve tremendous thanks before we acknowledge the wide-ranging contributions of others who have made the CTTL's journey possible. The good news is that after you read this curated collection of stories, you can also read those that had to be left out—as well as those that will be written in the years to come—at www.thecttl.org/think-differently-deeply.

All of the authors have busy jobs being teachers, parents, and students. We greatly appreciate that they took the time to write the stories that are all too rarely written in the world of education. Their articles for *Think Differently and Deeply* transformed how we think of ourselves as professional educators, and we thank them here for allowing us to share their stories together in this compendium.

The idea for *Think Differently and Deeply* emerged at St. Andrew's in 2011, and many people contributed to its creation and evolution. Nancy Schwartz provided considerable design help and invaluable feedback on the cover designs while Kirstin Petersen helped launch the *Think Differently and Deeply* podcast where you are able to hear some of the "live" voices of the authors. Our school leadership team played an important role in making *Think Differently and Deeply* a sustainable publication that could be broadly shared to educators, families, and decision-makers around the world. For that, we owe Robert Kosasky, the

Head of School at St. Andrew's, a debt of gratitude for his article title suggestions, and his own afterword to each edition. We appreciate his commitment to helping secure funding for the publication—including providing each contributing author a small stipend as a token of thanks for the time and effort they put into writing and rewriting their research-informed stories.

Many researchers at the university level, or connected with evidence-informed organizations, appear in the pages of this publication. They are thanked or referenced in footnotes. Many of these have also shared their research through the CTTL's annual Science of Teaching and School Leadership Academy, by reviewing CTTL translation materials, by helping us build new tools to support the research to classroom-to-student translation process, or by giving their time to talk to us about what the world of research-to-practice translation in education could look like.

We would like to particularly thank Dr. David Daniel and Dr. Mark McDaniel, whom we consider mentors and friends, for their help in the design of Neureoteach Global Student. Dr. Mariale Hardiman, Professor Emeritus at Johns Hopkins' School of Education, for providing us with some early ways to think about the potential of being a teacher-led, school-based research center with an international public purpose, and for her support and mentorship as the CTTL began and grew. A host of other individuals have helped us develop a doable, evidence-informed, evidence-generating process for bringing the science of teaching and learning into schools: in the United States, we would like to particularly thank Beth Morling, Kristen Gagnier, Kelly Fisher, Christina Hinton, Dan Willingham, Julie Jungalwala, Sheila Walker, Denise Pope, Dylan Wiliam, and Meg Lee; and in Europe, David Weston, Pedro de Bruckeye, Stuart Kime, Bradley Busch, and Rob Coe. You have all helped us think better about our work and how it can be shared in ways that are efficacious and responsible.

Funding has also been important to the CTTL's work, including making *Think Differently and Deeply* geographically and economically accessible. We would like to thank the Chan Zuckerberg Initiative, Crimsonbridge Foundation, EE Ford Foundation, and the Omidyar Group, each of whom recognized the importance of supporting our ongoing work to provide models of evidence-informed teaching and learning and helping other schools transform their work with every student. We imagine a world where every student has an expert teacher in every class, every day; your support takes us steps closer to that dream. We would also like to extend a huge thank you to the Dreyfuss, Demas, Finn, Harrison, Guerin-Calvert, and Smith families. Each of these St. Andrew's families has been an intellectual and philanthropic partner in the growth of the CTTL's team, its workspaces on the St. Andrew's campus, and its efforts to support teachers and school leaders in all educational settings through the development of innovative tools, experiences, and publications. In addition, each of the chairs of the CTTL Advisory Board, Dr. Jim Young, Noelle Eder, Kevin Borgman, and Brian Harris, have helped keep the CTTL focused on its internal to St. Andrew's and external to the larger educational community mission: "A world where every teacher understands how every student's brain learns."

As editors of *Research-Informed Teaching*, we each feel privileged to have brought this collection of educator-written, student-centered stories to life with the amazing and very patient team at John Catt. Their author-friendly process and steady support have allowed us to fit this writing project into our everyday work at St. Andrew's collaborating with our colleagues and teaching students.

Finally, a dual thank you—to the families and students we work with daily and to our amazing colleagues at St. Andrew's. You have motivated and supported us on every step of our journey. This book is written in honor of you. This is a book about great teaching. It is also a book inspired by the belief that every child around the world deserves a great teacher. Using the best evidence from research on what actually works to inform what we do each day has to be a part of how we get there.

Introduction

In 2007, our school explored this generative question: "How do we take good teachers and make them great and great teachers and make them expert?" As you can imagine, we came up with several potential answers. We need to elevate our understanding and use of Culturally Responsive Pedagogy, deepen our integration of technology, expand project based and experiential learning, provide better feedback, and measure growth through standards-based student portfolios. All great ideas, and all things that we have worked diligently on since. But we were also intrigued by a question that few people were asking at the time. **How many educators have ever read a book, attended a conference, or pursued college or graduate work in how the brain learns?** When we asked our colleagues back then, we found that roughly only 20% had.

It is quite an irony, isn't it? The brain is the organ of learning, after all. And there might be only one indisputable education truth—every day, every student, in every school and district will have their brain. So, shouldn't all teachers and school leaders understand the science behind how the brain learns, works, changes, and thrives? We know this is far from the case. We have asked our question to educators all over the world, and the same value of roughly 20% seems to hold true wherever we have gone. Few teachers anywhere have studied how the brain learns at a level that would elevate their effectiveness, their students' achievement, and the whole child's academic, social, emotional and identity development.

For us back in 2007, we saw that 20% value as an opportunity. It led our school to make a strategic decision—we were going to train 100% of our current *and future* teachers and administrators in the science of teaching learning, or what is often called mind, brain, and education (MBE). The biggest challenge was how would we do it? At the time, there were only two programs we were aware of that could (1) help us elevate our faculty's understanding of how the brain learns, works, changes; and (2), provide us with a common language and framework for this: The *All Kinds of Minds Neurodevelopmental Framework for Learning* (NDFL) and the *Brain-Targeted Teaching* (BTT) model developed by Johns Hopkins School of Education professor Dr. Mariale Hardiman. We chose the former after piloting the program with our middle school teachers and found it to be a good primer in the core concepts of neurodiversity.

This collective experience led to an increase in our teachers' collective sense of efficacy, their instructional variation, and their belief that all students can learn. Our conversations about teaching and learning changed and became more growth- and asset-based. We also recognized that teaching is both an art and a science, and the goal is not to base our teaching on research—following exactly the methods laid out in research papers. Rather, it is to *inform* our teaching with research—mixing insights from research with our own individual and collective professional wisdom, and coming up with practices that make sense for our unique context, our subject, our community, our students, and each of our unique voices as a teacher.

In doing this translational work we faced two challenges. First, how do we sustain this school-wide initiative to train, and keep training, 100% of our teachers and school leaders in MBE? Second, how, as an independent school with a public purpose, do we share and make accessible what we are learning about MBE integration so that public, charter, international, and private schools can consider how to use promising research and strategies in their context with their students?

In 2011, we launched the Center for Transformative Teaching and Learning (CTTL) to be the science of teaching and learning hub of the school—its research and professional development arm, if you will. the CTTL's focus was to "keep the foot on the gas" for this initiative. We shared research-informed strategies, and designed professional learning experiences and teacher-friendly *next-day-usable* resources for our colleagues. Promising principles of MBE were tried out in real classrooms by real teachers with real students. We got insights from all parties, iterated the tools we made, and tried again. And again. We also made the tools we created available to the global educational community. Every child everywhere benefits when their teachers are informed by insights from the science of teaching and learning. Our MBE Strategies Roadmaps for Early Childhood and Elementary Teachers, MBE Strategies Placemat for secondary and collegiate educators, Neuroteach Global online microcourses, and MythBusting card deck are now being used by teachers, schools, and districts around the world.

Also in 2011, we made one of our best decisions ever. We decided to collect, share, and honor stories of mind, brain, and education in action—our publication, *Think Differently and Deeply* was born. Teachers and students at our school became published authors. We shared field-tested research-informed strategies around neuroplasticity, attention, cognitive load, memory, metacognition, play, formative and summative assessment, feedback, spatial thinking, stress, sleep, mindsets for learning, social cognition, literacy, student agency, belonging, and more. We asked our colleagues to write two-page research-informed stories chronicling how they selected a strategy based on a need, challenge, or learning objective, what they actually did, and the impact it had. It may be focused on one student, five students, the entire class, or the whole school. We also provided a small stipend to each author to honor the time they gave to this endeavor on top of their other teaching responsibilities, and we threw a really special book launch party to honor their work.

Since our first volume of *Think Differently and Deeply* in 2011, there has been an explosion of research and resources in the science of teaching and learning and the field of MBE. We are grateful for those individual researchers we have had the chance to collaborate with, such as Mary Helen Immordino-Yang, Christina Hinton, Dan Willingham, Dylan Wiliam, Mariale Hardiman, the late Kurt Fischer, Pooja Agarwal, Denise Pope, Mark McDaniel, Adele Diamond, Vanessa Rodriguez, Tracey Tokuhama Espionosa, Rob Coe, Stuart Kime, Pedro de Bruyckere, Bob Dillon, Kristin Gagnier, Sandra McGuire, Kelly Fisher, Chris Hulleman, Gregg Dunn, Laura-Ann Petitto, Nicole Furlonge, and David Daniel, and organizations such as the Teacher Development Trust, Deans for Impact, Evidenced Based Education, Challenge Success, Learning & the Brain

Foundation, IMBES, Education Endowment Foundation, Turnaround for Children, ResearchEd, Wellcome Trust, and the Global Science of Learning Education Network. Keep the research coming!

We chose to pull together these *Think Differently and Deeply* stories to inspire teachers from grade- to graduate school. Can you leverage the most promising research and strategies in the science of teaching, learning, and development to help all students every day? As a community of educators, can we impact children in every classroom, regardless of school type or school location, or a student's race, ethnicity, social class, gender, sexual orientation, religion, or ability? Can we move toward a future where all teachers understand the science behind how the brain learns, works, changes, and thrives? Our children deserve this.

As you work through this book, listen to how all stakeholders in a student's education, including students themselves, are talking about how research in how the brain learns is informing and transforming their thinking and practice. Look for themes. Look for similar ideas appearing in different locations. Look for ways in which your own practices are validated— but also for ways in which you can tweak or transform what you do. Be inspired to be an agent for research-informed change.

Finally, we also hope that this book serves as a model for your school, program, or organization to create its own version of *Think Differently and Deeply*. This is our challenge to you. Engage in the transformative work of using research to inform your practice, collect the stories, and honor them in a way befitting this new vision of what it means to be a professional educator. Every child everywhere deserves teachers who know how the brain learns best.

Enjoy!

HOW TO USE THIS BOOK

There are many ways to enjoy this book. Read it through or:

Browse by subject: See what people are doing in your subject or a subject that has similar traits as yours.

Browse by strategy: Interested in belonging? Or formative assessment? Find some stories that line up with your interest, but also allow yourself to get distracted by other stories.

If you are reading this on your own...

After reading a story that resonates with you, try using capture, validate, change, share to help you unpack it and turn it into something useful.

1. **Capture**: Try to capture your insights from the story in three words. To reduce your cognitive load for the next steps, write them down.

2. **Validate**: Try to find one thing in your current practice that is validated by what you have just read. Keep doing this. But think about how you might tweak your current practice based on what you just read to make it even better.

3. **Change**: Find one thing in the article that might work in your class or school. Which lesson, unit, project, or part of the school would it live in? How would you have to adapt it to make it work in your unique context?

   Once you have done this, go into red-flag mode. Is there anything in the story that made you think, "maybe I shouldn't be doing this?" If you have an inkling that there is, explore this further. Try stopping the practice, tweaking it, or replacing it with something else and see what happens.

4. **Share**: When trying to implement a change in your class or school, it is helpful to have someone to bounce ideas off, be an ally in your work, or a go-to shoulder when things aren't going well. So, think about who you might share a copy of the story with. Get them to read it and talk with them about what you think is validated and what you might change.

If you are reading this as a group...

1. Give people some time to look through the contents, browse some stories, and find one that resonates with them. Write the title large and legibly on an index card or sticky-note.

2. Give people time to read the article they chose.

3. Get people to stand up, move around the room, and find someone who either has the same story as you, or a story that you think jigsaws together well. Groups of 3 are allowed—use your judgment.

4. Each pair or group discusses what they took from their story. Prompt them to talk about (a) what made them choose this story; (b) what was validated by this story; (c) what they are interested in starting to do; and, (d) is there anything about what they are currently doing that the story questions?

5. Each group has probably talked about many good things. Finish up by selecting one to share out. Here is one suggestion for doing this:

   As a group, try completing these two sentences, which could be shared back to the whole group in the format of your choice.

   To help our students _____, **we could try** _____.

   To see how well this is working we could look for/at _____.

6. Have a gallery walk. Afterward ask the whole room, what themes emerged from your gallery walk? What seems like an imperative? What really fits the mission of our school?

A FIVE-POINT PLAN FOR RESEARCH-INFORMED CHANGE IN CLASSROOMS, SCHOOLS, AND DISTRICTS

Step 1: Find a need. This could be an area of challenge for some or all your students. But it could also be an area of opportunity—are there any mission-level goals that your school is working on right now? Are there any large projects that you are about to plan? Is there something your students are okay at but that you just know could still be improved? All these are areas where a research-informed strategy could help.

Step 2: Choose a general MBE promising principle that might help you.
For example, cognitive load, sense of belonging, metacognition, feedback,
study strategies, literacy, play, mindsets for learning, motivation, teaching
and assessing in multiple modalities, or eliminating classroom threats.
You might need to read up about this—for suggestions visit thecttl.org
and see our Research Base.

Step 3: Translate it into everyday actions. MBE research does not give
you a cookbook answer. You need to make it work in your unique context,
and you need to combine insights from research with insights that no
researcher knows about—where you are the expert. Alongside the insights
from research, think about your own professional wisdom and that of
your colleagues. And think about your own secret sauce as a teacher—
what exactly makes awesome you awesome you? Put all these things into
the blender and come up with a plan that works for your students, your
school, your subject, your community, your personal voice as a teacher.

Step 4: Think about impact. Before putting your plan into action, think
about some things you might "measure" to see how it is going. "Measure"
does not have to mean you are counting something or giving your
students surveys (though it could). It just means that you are going to
be deliberate about watching what happens when you try your plan out.
Every teacher collects a huge amount of informal evidence all the time, it
is just part of the minute-to-minute job we do. All we are asking you to do
is to be a bit more deliberate about what you are looking for as markers of
how well your plan is working.

Step 5: Try your plan out, then iterate. Look for evidence of what is
working and what is not. Then, really, really importantly, **iterate** what
you do. That is, think about what tweaks, large or small, you could make
to improve this strategy the next time you try it. Go back to step 3, then
find a way to try your revised strategy again. And iterate some more.
Talk with colleagues about what you are doing and get their input as you
iterate—teacher wisdom alongside MBE research insights is where the
magic happens.

One last step! As you do all this, we think that you will probably create
your own story of MBE in action, one worthy of sharing. So, our challenge
to you is this. Write your own *Think Differently and Deeply* style article,

800–1200 words in a chatty style. And as you think about ways to share it out in your community, remember to send a copy to us: email it to info@ saes.org. We look forward to hearing from you!

Part I

Who Are We Doing This For: Student Voice and Student Agency

A Student Recall

Why should teachers and school leaders reconsider how they currently design their academic day? Why should educators use project-based learning (PBL), formative assessments, and multiple modality instruction? Why should schools develop a social and emotional curriculum, re-evaluate homework, and reconsider how students are assessed?

These strategies stem from mind, brain, and education (MBE) science, which can inform how educators enhance teacher quality to close the student achievement gap. Given that the organ of learning is the brain, one may assume that training and ongoing professional development in the learning brain would be a prerequisite for any educator. Unfortunately, such foundational MBE science training is not the case.

The CTTL partners with public, charter, private, state, and international schools. In fact, in each of the MBE science snapshot surveys the Center for Transformative Teaching and Learning conducts with teachers from its partner schools, one thing has remained constant: approximately 75% of teachers surveyed lacked the 30-hour threshold for MBE science training we have for 100% of the St. Andrew's preschool through 12th grade faculty and administration.

Through our presentations and workshops to more than 10,000 teachers and school leaders from around the world, we have discovered the strong demand for this knowledge; educators crave training regarding how to translate MBE research into practice. And research suggests that developing an educator's MBE knowledge, skills, and mindsets enhances their efficacy.[1] This, then, is a gateway for improving learning outcomes for all students.

Speaking from my own experience, I know that I am an exponentially better teacher today than I was when I first taught history in 1991 because of my training and ongoing professional development in mind, brain, and education science. I am a more effective educator than I was even five years ago due to my increasing knowledge of MBE science and experience translating that research. Moreover, I believe in my ability to better challenge and support each student, and I am having more fun in the classroom than ever before.

Therefore, I am declaring a recall of all my former St. Andrew's students. Whether I taught you Geography 6, AP US History, historical methods, comparative political economy, or United States/European history, I ask you to clear your schedules for a year to retake my class.

This recall is not because my students were not successful. Most of them succeeded because of their hard work ethic, and this was before any of us had heard of Carol Dweck's research on growth mindset, Angela Duckworth's work around grit and character, or the Mindset Scholars Network.[2] My students successfully drew a world map by heart, scored highly on AP exams, and produced essays or oral history projects that met scholarly standards. However, my former students would benefit from my increased understanding of the brain: how it works, learns, and thrives.

So, for my former students, what can you expect? Remember that time you pulled the "all-nighter" for the Cold War Period LOPP ("learning opportunity", my term for test), but the next morning you could not recall much of what you tried to embed in your long-term memory? I now have a better awareness of how emotions, sleep, and identity impact cognitive functions; I would coach you to space your studying so that you could retain and recall more historical knowledge.

---

1   Hardiman, M., Rinne, L., John Bull, R., Gregory, E., and Yarmolinskaya, J. (2013). "Professional Development Effects on Teacher Efficacy: Exploring How Knowledge of Neuro- and Cognitive Sciences Changes Beliefs and Practice." Paper presented at the American Educational Research Association conference, San Francisco, CA.

2   See: Dweck, C. (2007) *Mindset: The New Psychology of Success*. Ballantine Books. See also: The Mindset Scholars Network (mindsetscholarsnetwork.org).

Need help memorizing the history terms on those LOPPs? I will no longer merely suggest that you use flashcards; instead, I will encourage you to test yourself since active retrieval is an effective memory strategy.[3] In class, I will provide you with formative assessments to practice recalling the three S's of the Civil War Period, the five I's of the Progressive Period, or the twelve causes of the Great Depression.

Remember when your LOPP signaled the end of our unit? Now, before moving on to the next unit, you will complete "test" corrections and use metacognitive opportunities to reflect on your current strengths and weaknesses. Throughout this process, I will make sure you constantly experience struggle while feeling supported in the "zone of proximal discomfort."[4] For the visual artists I taught, I have created assessments that will allow you to use those strengths to demonstrate your knowledge of historical events. And yes, the amount of homework I give has lessened. I would like to think that the homework is not only less, but also better.

Teachers who understand the brain recognize that they can lower the barriers that every student faces in his or her learning journey. As an MBE research-informed teacher, I have realized that by reducing the barriers I am actually able to raise the bar for each one of my students. So, former students, what do you say?

3   See: The Learning Scientists (learningscientists.org) and Brown, P. C., Roediger III, H. L. and McDaniel, M. (2014). *Make It Stick: The Science of Successful Learning.* Belknap Press.
4   Whitman, G. and Kelleher, I. (2016). *Neuroteach: Brain Science and the Future of Education.* Rowman & Littlefield, 126.

Glenn Whitman is the Dreyfuss Family Director of the Center for Transformative Teaching and Learning at St. Andrew's (www.thecttl .org) and co-author of *Neuroteach: Brain Science and the Future of Education.*

The Roots of Student Success

In 2002, I graduated from St. Andrew's and went to Duke University on a soccer scholarship. Most people who attend Duke come from schools like St. Andrew's; however, in my freshman year writing seminar, I was paired with a girl who was not as fortunate. We had to turn in a paper as a pair. We each took a stab at different sections. When she sent me her part, it was immediately clear to me that she did not experience the rigor and instruction that I had from attending St. Andrew's in middle and high school.

Her sentences were run-ons, her writing was unclear; there was no structure. She was not able to write clearly and logically, a skill that I learned early on and completely took for granted. It was at this moment that I realized the exceptional quality of the education I received in those formative 7–12 grade years. Essentially, St. Andrew's gave me the foundation to be successful at Duke academically by providing me with an exceptional education and teaching me how I learn best.

St. Andrew's allowed me to discover my learning strengths and allowed my friends to do the same. It is a place where all types of learners can develop. I left high school as a successful learner and with the knowledge of how I learn best. That resulted in a continuous desire to learn and develop. This is a desire I still have today, and it has been at the forefront of my career decisions.

The quality of my high school education motivated me to join Teach For America after getting my undergraduate degree. In college, I realized how important education is to a person's success. Some of my peers, who were not as fortunate as I was, were at an academic disadvantage at Duke.

Despite that, they were likely going to be successful in their chosen careers because they earned a college degree from an exceptional university. It really troubled me that some children would be at a disadvantage in high school if they didn't have a good middle school education, and behind in middle school if they didn't have a good elementary school education.

Would these children ever even make it to college? It didn't seem right that because my parents were financially able to send me to an academically rigorous school, and others' parents are not, I got a better education that allowed me to get into Duke and thrive. I joined Teach For America because I believe that a great education is a civil right, and an equalizer.

After teaching I continued my education and earned an MBA. In my post-MBA position, I learn and develop each day—something that is necessary for my career—a mindset that I first developed while at St. Andrew's.

Carolyn Ford is a 2002 graduate of St. Andrew's and earned an undergraduate degree from Duke University. After serving in Teach For America, Carolyn earned an MBA from Duke's Fuqua School of Business.

I remember what I hear. This type of learning is rare. Studies show that people remember only 10% of what they hear, 30% of what they read, but 80% of what they see.[5] I fall into that first category. Specifically, I remember voices. These voices are a common thread connecting each step of my educational journey.

It was at St. Andrew's that I began to truly listen to these voices and in doing so learned that the critical difference between a degree and an education is measured by how we act upon what we learn. I continue to benefit from St. Andrew's mission to "know and inspire" each child, for it helped cultivate, support, and encourage my own unique learning style. This learning style of listening to the voices around me can be summarized in an education equation of sorts: knowledge + inspiration = positive change.

---

5   Jerome Bruner, as cited by Paul Martin Lester in "Syntactic Theory of Visual Communication," California State University at Fullerton, 1994–1996.

The first voices I encountered at St. Andrew's were inside the classroom. Confronted by a break to my dominant arm in middle school, one of my teachers suggested I take notes and tests with a tape recorder. He quelled my fears of receiving special treatment by explaining that my education was not just for me, but for those I would impact in the future. In contrast to an anticipated decline in grades, my newly acquired auditory study skills propelled me into a new place academically. I not only learned how I learned best, but I came to love what I learned. Compounded with this newfound understanding of my learning style, I was encouraged by my teachers to listen closely, think critically, and respond creatively to issues and questions that arose in the classroom. In classes that I gravitated toward, as well as those I struggled in, I found my teachers patient and willing to help me better understand. I am grateful to those voices, for now I recognize how the St. Andrew's faculty used theirs to inspire students to better understand the world around us.

The second type of voices St. Andrew's encouraged me to listen to were those outside the classroom. My most memorable classes were those that bridged the lessons in my books with people and events outside of the classroom. The Oral History Project encouraged me to absorb the words of civil rights activists and social justice trailblazers—the voices of Americans who had lived lives of knowledge translated into action. The Race & Culture class featured service learning and exchange between students of not only different schools, but different continents, and broadened my perspective by introducing me to voices of courage, social change, and hope that I carry with me to this day. Service opportunities, such as the senior project, helped humanize issues and tools I learned about in class and put them in a modern-day context. This way of learning continually emphasizes that knowing is not enough but coupled with inspiration, it is a catalyst to contribute positively to the wider community.

Finally, St. Andrew's encouraged me to listen to voices beyond the classroom. In college, I was well prepared to listen critically and respond constructively to the voices around me—through classes, extracurricular activities and, direct service. On a volunteer trip for hurricane relief during my freshman year in college, a classmate and I were motivated by the voices of survivors. We put together a campus organization providing female students a space to add their voice to the political dialogue. After graduation, at an international non-profit, I learned to listen to and advocate for the voices of female human rights survivors and activists from around the world.

Now in law school, I am determined to become a better advocate—to use my voice to amplify the voices of those who can only whisper.

Above all, St. Andrew's taught me how to listen. While the auditory learner in me prefers listening to speaking, beginning at St. Andrew's, listening to voices galvanized me to find and use my own. In doing so, St. Andrew's bridged the gap between knowledge and action, through inspiration. In this way, I learned that the substance of what I learn and process through which I learn it are inextricably connected; knowing is about the substance of what I learn, and being inspired is how I seek to translate this knowledge into positive change.

Nicole Hauspurg is a 2005 graduate of St. Andrew's and earned an undergraduate degree from Georgetown University.

St. Andrew's, Yale, and My Prefrontal Cortex

Ms. Racquel Yerbury, my former Latin teacher and eternal friend, was quite fond of the Socratic method. As our five-person AP Latin class took turns deciphering Virgil's *The Aeneid*, she would periodically interrupt with a guiding question: "What noun must this adjective agree with?" "Where's the verb?" "What is the context of this sentence?" I found such inquiries immensely helpful in a course that frequently tests (and frustrates) the most dedicated classicists.

And then there is my English teacher, Mr. Morgan Evans, with whom I spent countless hours discussing my senior thesis. When I say "discuss," I mean debating, analyzing, and philosophizing about the confluence of economic and intellectual history in Western Europe, not scanning for punctuation errors or sentence fragments. We spoke almost as colleagues, and our conversations invariably devolved into the most profound and tangential of meditations.

Neither of the above techniques is particularly new. Antiquity adopted Ms. Yerbury's strategy well before St. Andrew, our patron Saint, set foot on earth, and tutorials have existed at Oxford since the 15th century. What is new—and, I think, quite exciting—is how St. Andrew's has incorporated these teaching methods into its academic milieu.

Regardless of what school you attend, lectures and in-class activities can only go so far toward refining your writing and analytical abilities. Rigorous, personalized feedback is essential for growth irrespective of grade-point average, and St. Andrew's is unparalleled in this respect. Teachers consistently display an astonishing eagerness to engage with and befriend students. For what we might call more gifted students, these types of interactions are especially valuable. A constant stream of difficult questions in class or a provocative observation about a paper will always force smart, motivated scholars to go one step further, to think, in the highest sense of the words, differently and deeply.

Metacognition is the process by which one reflects on his or her own mind to develop one's optimal learning strategies. For me, metacognition meant engaging with my teachers both in and outside of the classroom, thinking about a challenging question until I could reply with an even tougher one. My teachers never discouraged me from pursuing dialectical inquiry, nor did they recoil when I posed a question to which they did not know the answer. On the contrary, they redoubled their efforts to baffle and delight me with new investigations.

I write this article on the eve of my matriculation at Yale, where I will be enrolling in a selective program devoted to an intensive study of Western literature, political thought, and philosophy. I can't tell you what grade I will get on my first paper, or how long it will take for me to complete my first problem set in calculus. But I can tell you that I feel very prepared (and excited) to spar with my future classmates, accomplished though they will be. I discovered at St. Andrew's a singular passion for ideas, for disagreement, for dialogue. That is true critical thinking, and few schools could have possibly taught it as successfully as this one has.

For that, St. Andrew's, I cannot possibly thank you enough.

Aaron Sibarium is a 2014 graduate of St. Andrew's and earned an undergraduate degree from Yale University.

From Failing at St. Andrew's to Failing at Stanford

On a typical winter day during my first year at Stanford, my Psychology One professor began class by posting a Carol Dweck quote on the board: "Becoming is better than being." My peers cocked their heads and narrowed their eyes, puzzled over how the quote by Stanford's renowned psychologist related to the lecture's topic of intelligence. Yet it instantly clicked with me.

On my first day at St. Andrew's in 2009, the Dean of Studies strode in front of the disjointed, awkward bunch of pre-teens to champion a Stanford psychologist's emerging theory. He sternly held up a framed poster, with two simple words in boldface at the top: growth mindset.

This teacher, who I later learned was Glenn Whitman, explained that those who hold a growth mindset believe intelligence can change through one's effort, one's process, and one's experiences. Although, he remarked, most people still hold an antithetical mindset, called the fixed mindset, we have the agency to change our beliefs, and thus alter the course of how we think and act. In essence, Mr. Whitman proclaimed that we—not our luck, our environment, nor our genes—could decide our futures. And the thought of that power was both terrifying and exhilarating. But harnessing that power isn't just up to the individual; in reality, it relies on the work of a community.

Each teacher I encountered at St. Andrew's truly believed I could succeed, for the growth mindset was built into the framework of the institution. We earned effort grades alongside academic ones, athletes were recognized for their improvement more than anything else, and each student was required to challenge themselves by taking an art course. From cross-country to Spanish, I struggled, wriggled, failed, and bounced back, but those struggles were most pronounced in writing.

I am not a natural writer. As a middle schooler, typing anything longer than a paragraph paralyzed me, and by ninth grade my essays still consisted of simple sentences using various conjugations of the verb "to be." Each school year my most dreaded subject remained English, and I couldn't fathom how I would tackle the beast known as the senior paper. And although every English and history teacher I had inched my capabilities along, my writing progressed by leaps and bounds my junior year because of AP English and my teacher, Morgan Evans.

With a booming voice, dynamic hand gestures, and frazzled note-taking, Mr. Evans exuded an aura of zeal for the books we were reading that made you want to learn. During our first few in-class discussions, I felt that every comment I posited was swiftly crushed by Mr. Evans's and my classmates' superior ideas. On my first essay, I received the lowest mark I had on any paper to date. But Mr. Evans's love of teaching galvanized me to want to learn.

I began meeting with Mr. Evans outside of class—during break, after school, even during lunch—to work on my papers. Although my academic grades did not immediately improve, Mr. Evans commended me with higher effort marks. And as I persisted, Mr. Evans noticed and reciprocated. When the senior paper came knocking at my door a year later, I knew I would triumph.

By then, Mr. Whitman had led the founding of the Center for Transformative Teaching and Learning (CTTL), whose mission is to use mind, brain, and education science to "allow teachers to maximize their effectiveness and students to achieve their highest potential." As part of one of his campaigns to disseminate the ideas of the CTTL, Mr. Whitman created t-shirts proudly displaying the word "yet" in large font, and, as a side note underneath, added "it's our mindset." While he went on to explain this "mindset" to the whole school in a talk at chapel, all I could envision was the poster from sixth grade that still hung by the middle school entrance.

Since coming to Stanford, I've had countless "yet" experiences. I've tried half a dozen different clubs—the Stanford Band, Cardinal Calypso, Fascinate Magazine, Queer Liberation, Stanford Kenpo, Students for a Sustainable Stanford—all of which I've quit. At the halfway point of the first quarter, I found myself struggling in my first STEM class at Stanford, Intro to Chemistry. To this day, I haven't declared a major, and my advisor lovingly compares my schedule to a poor player's darts on a dartboard.

But along the way, I've grown. I've fallen in love with a few student organizations that now mean a lot to me, and have a list of others I want to try this coming school year. After venturing to office hours and requesting a tutor, my grades in Chemistry began to improve. And although I haven't set my heart on a major quite yet, I have some pretty good ideas that I plan to explore more deeply.

Despite the uncertainty of freshman fall, there was one thing I could count on: succeeding in my writing seminar. While many of my peers moaned over writing more than three pages, I welcomed the assignments as old friends. Right off the bat, my instructor informed me my work was some of the best in the class, and at the end of the quarter recommended that I submit my research paper to a school-wide competition. I smiled when she said this, recalling the senior paper, Mr. Evans, and countless other teachers I'd had at St. Andrew's who helped me get to that point.

While I have put in the hours studying, reading, writing, taking risks, failing and trying again, I've had St. Andrew's with me every step of the way.

Robyn Radecki graduated from St. Andrew's in 2016 and earned an undergraduate degree from Stanford University. While at St. Andrew's, Robyn was a CTTL/Finn Student Research Fellow.

The Teenage Brain

Behind each of my cartoons, I try to insert an underlying and relatable truth. For an image that would be used on the cover of the CTTL workbook for its Science of Teaching and School Leadership Academy, I was told that I should aim to combine humor and subtle scientific accuracies in a drawing that would convey a goal of the CTTL: understanding the brain as a core part of teaching and learning.

So, I decided I would teach the audience a perspective of my own.

First came the sketch. What came to my mind? A huge brain. Not just any brain, but a hectic, glorious student brain: a brain drawn from my experiences as a teenager, a scholar, and a CTTL/Finn Student Research Fellow. In attempting to sketch a human brain and drawing what looked like a dehydrated lima bean, I quickly realized that I was very rusty on my neurological scientific anatomy. Refusing to admit that I was a CTTL fellow finding myself in this position, I quickly turned to the internet for detailed brain diagrams. I found hundreds. Before I knew it, I was enjoying a self-taught lesson on the parts and regions of my own mind, becoming absorbed in the complexities and conveniences of its remarkable design.

I first drew out several factual parts and regions of the brain. I was reminded that our capacity for rational thought is really guided by the prefrontal cortex region lying just behind our foreheads. Also, the fact that we all have a portion of the brain called the anterior cingulate that is dedicated entirely to motivation is fascinating. Most diagrams of the brain are so detailed, it's overwhelming, yet understanding the regions of our brain is crucial for education.

I considered just drawing my own labeled scientific diagram for the CTTL cover. But where's the fun in that? I was missing something. What about the portion of our student brains that craves a three-cheese pizza at midnight, or harbors hundreds of our favorite snippets of internet humor? What about wanderlust, spontaneous teenage wisdom, or the deeply rooted school spirit that emerges in our senior year of high school? I started drawing in these abstract, imaginative regions to capture both the teenage mind and soul. My sketch combined factual regions such as the hippocampus, amygdala, and prefrontal cortex, with my fictional regions, such as "Memory Lane" or the "iForgot Zone." A traffic light, a hippo, a monkey with cymbals, and, yes, a fidget spinner, all took form in my diagram.

After a few hours spent drawing and inhaling the fumes of permanent markers, I had transferred the sketch into a final inked form and uploaded it to Photoshop. As the CTTL would say, I was not proficient with Photoshop...yet. I decided it was time to teach myself the skill. Finally, and victoriously, I succeeded in blocking in a simple psychedelic pastel color scheme to my brain drawing. I experienced firsthand another central message of the CTTL: our brains are not fixed to be "good" or "bad" at something indefinitely.

PARTS OF THE STUDENT BRAIN

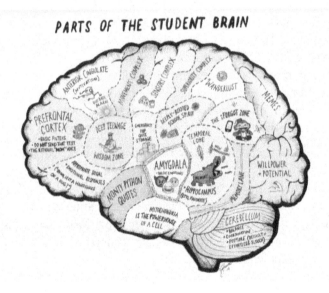

Overall, the opportunity to create a cartoon for the CTTL was one of the most rewarding parts of my summer of 2017. I hope that parents, teachers, students, and Academy attendees can all relate to my depiction of the animated, ridiculous, and remarkable Student Brain.

Joy Reeves graduated from St. Andrew's in 2018 where she was a CTTL/Finn Student Research Fellow and won the National Science Foundation's Generation Nano Award. Joy earned an undergraduate degree from Duke University.

Chasing Sleep

As a high schooler, I am constantly chasing sleep. In my role as a CTTL Student Research Fellow, I was asked to come to a meeting with teachers and talk about the research data we had collected on the school's new schedule. Our discussion soon turned to the topic of Time by Design, a feature of our new schedule. On select Wednesdays, about half of the ones occurring during the school year, classes start an hour later and students have the option of coming to school to participate in activities or sleep in and come to school an hour later than usual.[6] Some teachers told me they didn't understand giving kids this downtime if they didn't take advantage by participating in the activities offered, and instead used the time to sleep in and come to school late. That is when I spoke up and shared something that I believe is my truth, and probably the truth of many high school students: I am chasing sleep.

Sleep is a priority, yet too often for me, and other sleep-deprived teens, it falls to the wayside in favor of the never-ending to-do list, an attempt to balance our lives, without much of a margin for error. A never-ending sleep loss, being less efficient, staying up later to make up for it, and losing more sleep, has made a sleep-deprived insomniac of too many teens. While sleeping in one day during the school week doesn't necessarily make up for inadequate nights of sleep other days, it does promote, if not ensure, one night of healthy sleep. Teenagers' brains need 9-10 hours of sleep a night to function properly,[7] yet few actually reach this mark due to

---

6   "Time Is the Prize: Our Research-Informed Schedule" in *Think Differently and Deeply* (Vol 3) (2018).

7   Canadian Paediatric Society. (2008). "Teens and sleep: Why You Need It and How To Get Enough." *Paediatrics & Child Health*, 13(1), 69–70.

their environment. The lack of sleep affects teens' brains, academics, and lives; thus, it is crucial to re-work our school day to create an environment in which students can sleep well and finish the race for sleep.

Trying to balance schoolwork, activities, sports, work, family, friends, self-care (genuine me-time), and the college application process means that searching for sleep gets lost in the process. During my sophomore year, my English teacher once asked my class what our ideal bedtime was. Expecting an absurdly late hour, he was surprised when I, along with the other sleep-deprived teens that filled my class, answered 9 p.m. or 10 p.m. It's not that I don't want to get a good night's sleep—an early bedtime and 9 to 10 hours of sleep is my dream. It's that as a high school student, to get everything done, my schedule is one of early mornings, late nights, and 6 or 7 hours of sleep—which would be a good night. Often the total is below that. According to researchers, "Not only is a good night's sleep required to form new learning and memory pathways in the brain, but also sleep is necessary for those pathways to work well."[8]

Thus lack of sleep affects memory, decision making, attention span, and mood; causes the thinking process to slow, and confusion to arise. However, it doesn't take a neuroscientist to notice that when one is well-rested they work better and more effectively than when they are sleep deprived. When I'm well-rested I am more invested in class, I'm better at conveying my thoughts, I recall information quicker, I can manage my time better, and I'm less tired by the time I get to my homework. When I'm well-rested I'm a better student; thus, sleeping in the extra hour or so and taking a break isn't necessarily unproductive.

As my teachers Mr. Whitman and Dr. Kelleher said in their book, *Neuroteach*, a common myth about the brain is that when we sleep, the brain shuts down. The reality is that "the brain is still active when we sleep, and certain crucial brain tasks, including ones associated with memory storage, only happen during this time. Sleep is vital for learning."[9] In fact it's probably the best way to use my time. Thus, my failure in the eyes of

---

8   US Department of Health and Human Services, National Institute of Health. (November 2005). *Your Guide to Healthy Sleep*. https://www.nhlbi.nih.gov/files/docs/public/sleep/healthy_sleep.pdf.

9   Whitman, G. and Kelleher, I. (2016). *Neuroteach: Brain Science and the Future of Education*. Rowman & Littlefield Publishers.

teachers to sign up for more activities during Time by Design and opt to sleep in is, in my eyes, my success. While to some it may look like students are merely looking to do less work, sleep helps students do more quality work, and improve their mental health. Finally, in the race for sleep, I've gotten to a point where I can stop and catch my breath.

Sarah Schwartz graduated from St. Andrew's in 2020 and was named a *Bethesda Magazine* "Extraordinary Teen" for, in part, her activism around immigration. While at St. Andrew's, Sarah was a CTTL/Finn Student Research Fellow.

Going Big on Retrieval Practice

It was a boring Monday night in late May, and the three of us wanted to hang out after school. Our parents only agreed on one condition: that we would be productive and study for our upcoming exams. We explained that although our final exams were drawing near, we felt that we had studied for each one as best as we could using the exam review resources and guidelines provided to us by our teachers. What more could we do? In order to appease our parents, we had to figure out a study strategy that would be useful and effective; and to appease us, one that was also engaging and enjoyable. Quizlet, flashcards, self-testing, and referring back to class notes were all fine strategies, but we wanted to create one that would help us fully grasp all of the information needed for our final exams, as well as one that fit where we were mentally, having already done a lot of studying.

First, we had to pick a subject. We all had history class together so we felt that it would be the wisest decision to choose that course. Next, we had to collaborate to create an incredible, impeccable method for studying and learning the material, but whatever would we choose?

Maya mentioned that she had a large scroll of paper in her basement. Cece got excited because she happened to have some nice markers. Will posed the question of what we could create with this perfect storm of blank canvas and colored markers.

Eureka! The "colossal piece of paper" was born and we set off to create our study tool. We started by writing down historical words we needed to remember. We then recalled and wrote down the first 16 presidents of the United States. Next, we worked to recall from memory, and then by looking at our notes, the three historical chains of causation and the 22 Terms of the Historian. After that, we decided to make a table showcasing wars from the French-Indian War to the Civil War, and important information about them. We proceeded to list the acts and compromises in chronological order from the "Great Compromise" to the Compromise of 1850.

This technique for studying helped us tremendously on the final exam. As Dr. Kelleher , the CTTL's Head of Research has suggested, we learned more when we made ourselves think hard. It also validated the idea that studying for a test or exam is, as our teacher Mr. Whitman often said, a "learning opportunity (LOPP)." It helped Will remember the presidents, a topic he struggled with all year. Cece benefited from writing down lists of terms we needed to know. Maya, who struggled with remembering dates of the acts and compromises, was able to recall them during the exam.

It was also validating to see this way of studying reinforced by Dr. Pooja Agarwal and Patrice Bain in their book, *Powerful Teaching: Unleashing the Science of Learning*.[10] Maya experienced this firsthand during her experience in 2019 as an intern for the CTTL's Science of Teaching and Leadership Academy. The book's strategies—spacing effect, retrieval practice, self-testing—should be part of every student's study strategy tool kit, to be used when needed.

Our colossal retrieval practice project helped us learn a great deal about our learning, as well as the material covered in our history class. Memory and recall strategies were introduced to us at various points in the year by our teachers in order to help us prepare for tests and other LOPPs. The act of having frequent recall tests, that counted for few or no points, was a common feature in many classes. And our teachers routinely used different teaching methods in class to help us remember the information. All of this helped us gain the skills to use more active study strategies beyond the typical flashcards. Finding an active study strategy that works for you for this material was a common theme of our classes. Thus, when we faced the most comprehensive and stressful exam of the year, we had

---

10   Agarwal, P. K. and Bain, P. M. (2019). *Powerful Teaching: Unleash the Science of Learning*. Jossey-Bass.

strategy options to help us remember the information for the short term and for the future, and a mindset to figure out an effective strategy that was going to work for us.

Each of us—Maya, Cece, and Will—have different strengths in the way that we learn. Through this study experience, we learned that pooling our collective strengths can help us to collectively prepare for an exam while also having fun working hard with our friends. We did not do equally well on this 10th grade history final exam, but months after the exam we are still each able to recall much of what we spent retrieving that night.

Will Cirrito, Cece Fainberg, and Maya Noboa each graduated from St. Andrew's in 2021.

Developing Students' Voices

As a former college professor, there were several questions I would hear from my students, be they undergraduate, graduate, or postgraduate students: "How many pages should this paper be?" or, "What's the word count for this paper?" Despite my internal disdain for these questions, I would calmly respond with the same answer: "Your paper should be long enough to provide evidence that you understand the topic you are producing." Seeing that students were uneasy with this response as they realized they would have to use their critical thinking and active reading skills and bring their own perspective to achieve success on my assigned papers provided me with a sense of enjoyment and justification that I am in the right profession.

The root of my excitement relates to the notion that many of today's learners are conditioned to follow a rubric, which is both beneficial and problematic. The majority of my students prefer a rubric, primarily because this mechanism creates a more objective method of scoring and because they are clear on how they will be evaluated.[11] My issue with relying on a rubric is that I believe students can be less inclined to think critically or holistically about the purpose of the assignment—thereby losing the opportunity to explore their learning at the sake of only obtaining a passing grade. When this is common practice, I posit that students' voices, literacy, and perspectives can be muted as they simply navigate toward a grade, consequently impacting their development, self-confidence, and advancement in life.

---

11   Using Rubrics for Assessment. (2011). Retrieved from: https://sites.ualberta
     .ca/~obilash/rubrics.html.

Classes need to have student voice designed into them. Providing students with a space to voice their ideas "create[s] programs and policies that are more effective at meeting the school's own goals for supporting young people in their healthy development."[12] And while some of the places where student voice might be either incorporated or shut out are obvious, some, such as how we create rubrics, are perhaps not.

Below are some strategies I employ in my 11th grade English classes at St. Andrew's to develop, support, and advance students' voices on a consistent basis:

- Having students respond to statements, quotes, or current issues both orally and in writing.

- Engaging students in discussion about the learned material and its applicability to their everyday life and society at-large, as opposed to simply perusing through the curriculum.

- Avoiding closed-ended questions and posing open-ended questions, while also asking students to explain their responses in detail. I also ask their peers to provide their perspectives on the given response.

- Encouraging students to omit the word "it" from their writing and to explain what "it" is in relation to what they are trying to highlight.

- Not allowing students to regurgitate the material we are learning, but rather advocating for them to respond to prompts in their own words.

With anything new, there's always apprehension and a lack of confidence in one's ability to perform at the expected level, and they were present as I began using these strategies with my St. Andrew's students. Because we are a school that favors a growth mindset, coupled with me being unapologetic about having high expectations for my learners, I spent the first few weeks of the school year assuring my students that they were going to be okay and to trust the academic journey I was charging them with. Easier said than done, right?

---

12 Shafer, L. (2016). "Giving Students a Voice: Five Ways to Welcome Student Input and Bolster Your School's Success", Harvard Graduate School of Education, 18 August, https://www.gse.harvard.edu/news/uk/16/08/giving-students-voice.

"I just don't understand," argued a few students. "I'm just not used to this way of learning," mentioned another 11th grader, whose comment was echoed by a myriad of their contemporaries. All valid responses, but in staying true to the academic journey we were traveling, I constantly reminded each student who openly or non-verbally communicated their anxiety about how they will be evaluated in my class that the benefit in practicing these strategies would help them progress academically, socially, and professionally. These words of confirmation subsided some of their fears, which is an accomplishment considering the level of angst several of my students had upon adapting to my pedagogy.

Although not said to my students, the approach I instituted in my classroom aligned with 9 out of the 15 power strategies for teachers outlined in the CTTL's mind, brain, and education (MBE) Research-Informed Strategies Placemat. Specifically, these include and are explained as follows:

1) Moving beyond lecture, by engaging students and encouraging active learning during the times I am introducing material to the class. This is done by posing clarifying questions, having students think–pair–share, displaying images and videos to gauge students' perspective, and facilitating open discussions where all participate.

2) Connecting class to students' lives, where I focus on teaching students applicable skills and knowledge that can be used in their everyday life and beyond.

3) Including choice and play, by allowing students guided autonomy on acceptable projects they can complete for a grade.

4) Understanding the link between emotion and cognition, by encouraging students with positive words of affirmation to give them the self-confidence and motivation to play active roles in their learning.

5) Minimizing classroom threats, where I purposefully create a safe and respectful learning environment, where students feel comfortable expressing their ideas without fear of being judged.

6) Helping to grow executive functioning, by constantly using scaffolded activities to help students reflect on the learned material, along with their peers' responses to help students, and use these

insights to improve their work. I am also constantly working to reduce these scaffolds so that my students may become better independent learners.

7) Combining joy and rigor, where I am adamant about establishing positive student-teacher relationships, meeting my students at their current academic level, but rigorously challenging them to go beyond their comfort zone, and making the learning experience as pleasant as possible. It is a magic zone for learning where students are outside their comfort zone, but comfortable being there.

8) Building students' metacognition skills, which MBE research considers as a high-impact strategy;[13] I ask my students to not only reflect on and respond to what we are learning, but to also explicitly describe their analysis of the topic we are discussing, using the same skills and thinking routines that we have used before. My objective is to have students think about their own learning and connect their prior experiences in my class with what I am currently asking them to do.

9) Exploring beyond growth mindset, by tailoring my instruction to meet students' academic needs, while focusing on the quality of their effort, as opposed to their ability. Ideally, I am intentional about building one's self-confidence. Therefore, when assessing students, I give oral and written feedback to guide them through the academic challenges they are facing to ultimately help them self-identify their strengths and weaknesses, and give them opportunities to act on this feedback.

In a perfect world, each student will enter a teacher's classroom with the prerequisite skill sets to succeed academically, but that rarely happens. Building students' self-confidence and creating space to allow them to voice their opinions, whether good, bad, or indifferent, are strategies that can be instituted to prepare students for success in and out of the classroom.

I attest that if we as educators are employing the aforementioned strategies, we are preparing our students for the demands of the 21st-

---

13   Perry, J., Lundie, D. and Golder, G. (2019). "Metacognition in Schools: What Does the Literature Suggest About the Effectiveness Of Teaching Metacognition in Schools?", *Educational Review*, 71(4), 483–500.

century workforce and world that is interdependent and constantly evolving. Therefore, I challenge each educator who encounters a student who questions the length of an assigned paper, or one who swears they have nothing to talk about and doesn't know what to write to remind them with guided instruction that they have the autonomy to voice whatever is on their mind because their perspective is valued, and needed, not only for their progression in life, but also because of the learning opportunity that is afforded to their peers.

With gratitude, I am pleased to note that my St. Andrew's students are adapting to my demands. Rather than ask how long their paper should be, one student asked, "Dr. Waters, because you are not big on word count and page length, I want to ensure we'll be okay ... as long as we support our points with valid supporting evidence?"

I'm sure you can guess the response I gave.

Dr. Kenneth Waters taught English at St. Andrew's during the writing of this research-informed article. He was also the upper school Diversity Coordinator and coached basketball.

A Parent's Mind, Brain, and Education Science

My first brush with mind, brain, and education science was two weeks before my Cambridge A-level examinations in the early 1990s. I had unwrapped my biology textbook for the first time and was having a mind-shock moment realizing the amount of material I had to memorize on brain anatomy. I blame this predicament on my release from an all-girls middle school to a co-ed high school; my sensory memory was overloaded with walking males of the species that promptly hijacked my ability to executive function.

Fast forward to some decades later: my amygdala is screaming bloody murder. I am facing mind, brain, and education (MBE) all over again. My children attend St. Andrew's, a school that infuses research-informed MBE strategies into its learning environment, curriculum design, pedagogy, assessment, student success, and well-being.

WHAT IS MBE?

By definition, "mind, brain, and education" is an intersection of neuroscience, behavioral psychology, and education theory. Just writing that is so massively daunting. What exactly do all those components mean? How can a parent like me use these evidence-based practices and know just enough to help me do my job as a parent better?

THE BRIDGE BETWEEN EDUCATORS AND PARENTS

I found my answer in a book called *The Self-Driven Child* by Dr. William Stixrud and Ned Johnson.[14] While the school uses MBE in an educational setting, the authors of *The Self-Driven Child* explain the same MBE concepts in the context of motivation, fighting about homework, and being a non-anxious parent. This gives me the belief that there is a common block of research data that can be used as an interchangeable vocabulary between parents and educators. This is extremely powerful, as a large part of our child's growing years involve education. To be optimal partners with educators in raising our children, shared knowledge is desirable.

THE BRIDGE BETWEEN ALL YOUR KIDS

I am all for a universal cure and efficiency. So, I looked at my brood and concluded that the only common denominator among them is the fact that they have a brain. Amid their differing personalities, genders, ages and developmental stages, I figured that if I can work out what goes on in their heads, I have a better chance at success.

For example, take the concept of executive-functioning skills, i.e., the ability to devise an appropriate plan, execute it, self-monitor while doing so, make adjustments as necessary, and determine a satisfactory endpoint. MBE informs us that the part of the brain that controls this skill is only fully developed around 25-years-old. It also tells us that the more you use a part of the brain, the better you get at it.

As a parent, we know that helping to grow executive function for all our kids is essential. It is not an excuse that they aren't biologically unable to plan and complete a task, and thus we will sweep in to do it for them. Instead, I identify where they are in their current ability and help them where they need it. So, for my youngest who is 8, he gets a chance to practice by coming up with a daily to-do list. For the older children, I leave them to plan and organize on their own but I check and suggest better ways to get their tasks done. And when I see a 2-month-aged piece of moldy bread at the bottom of their bag, I cut them some slack and blame it on their under-developed brain.

---

14 Stixrud, W. R., Johnson, N. and Fair, J. D. (2019). *The Self-Driven Child: The Science and Sense of Giving Your Kids More Control Over Their Lives.* Penguin Books.

MY TWO BIGGEST MBE APPLICATIONS AS A PARENT

1. Parent as a Consultant: Child development experts, such as Madeline Levine[15] and Laurence Steinberg,[16] provide evidence that "Authoritative Parenting" produces the best outcomes.[17] It entails being supportive, but not controlling. The key is to give the kids all the resources they need to make an informed decision, and then allow them to learn from their own experiences. Based on this parenting concept, Stixrud and Johnson, authors of *The Self-Driven Child*, urge parents to act as consultants, instead of enforcers. Consultants provide support yet recognize that it is the client's responsibility. Whose problem is it? In this case, it is the child's.

So I learned that it is healthy to take a hands-off attitude and let my children struggle, but make sure to let them know that I am there for them when needed. This point is also outlined in the book *Neuroteach* which talks about finding the "zone of proximal discomfort" for each individual learner.[18]

2. The Power of Yet: Stanford University professor Carol Dweck explains that having a growth mindset as opposed to a fixed mindset will influence a student's academic achievement and his/her ability to think and work at the highest level in a resilient manner.[19] Glenn Whitman and Dr. Ian Kelleher, the authors of *Neuroteach*, went a step further to explain that to cultivate a growth mindset for our children, it is not replacing the words, "Good job!" with "Good effort!" When one is running on a hamster wheel with no strategy and help to get off it, effort doesn't help. They write that "having a growth mindset also requires the development of clearly-defined strategies for improvement and the enlistment of support, advice,

15   Levine, M. (2008). *The Price of Privilege: How Parental Pressure and Material Advantage Are Creating a Generation of Disconnected and Unhappy Kids*. HarperCollins.
16   Steinberg, L. D. (2015). *Age of Opportunity: Lessons from the New Science of Adolescence*. Houghton Mifflin Harcourt.
17   Lamborn, S. D., Mounts, N. S., Steinberg, L. and Dornbusch, S. M. (1991). "Patterns of Competence and Adjustment among Adolescents from Authoritative, Authoritarian, Indulgent, and Neglectful Families", *Child Development*, 62(5), 1049.
18   Whitman, G. and Kelleher, I. (2016). *Neuroteach: Brain Science and the Future of Education*. Rowman & Littlefield.
19   Dweck, C. S. (2006). *Mindset: The New Psychology of Success*. Random House.

and guidance from others." In short, you cannot have a growth mindset without a challenge.

If they have no insight or plans on how to improve, trying their best won't be enough. I need to help them brainstorm, apply, test, and tweak strategies in their learning process. And in the midst of this all, I remind them that they sometimes just can't do it yet. Dweck's research is often over-simplified to "have a *you-can-do-it!* attitude." People miss the most important piece of her work, that quality of effort and using good strategies are vital.

I did well enough on my A-level biology examinations to get into college with my spot-the-questions strategy. But as MBE will tell you, I learned and retained nothing from those two weeks of cramming. But hey, at least high school was fun and if I had to do it all over again, I now have the research-informed strategies to make it stick longer.

Priscilla Ang is a parent of three children who attended St. Andrew's and she experienced firsthand the impact the CTTL has on a school when it commits to research-informed teaching and learning from kindergarten through grade 12.

Part II

Early Childhood and Elementary: A Research-Informed Head Start for Our Youngest Learners

It All Begins in Preschool

Last year, our kindergarten teacher asked me if our preschool classroom would like to have their play kitchen. Our well-loved kitchen had seen better days, so I happily accepted her offer. As I moved our newly upgraded kitchen (with refrigerator and microwave!) into its spot in our classroom, it suddenly occurred to me how much kindergarten has changed since I was in school.

In 1972, I attended a half-day program where the curriculum consisted primarily of unstructured free play, naptime, and crafting, with a little formal instruction thrown in for good measure. Today, most kindergarteners attend a full-day program, and while it is still fun and exciting with plenty of crafts, story time, and free play, it is also much more challenging academically with more classroom time devoted to formal instruction in reading, math, science, social studies, and the arts. I don't point out these differences to be critical of what kindergarten has become over the years, but it does serve as a reminder of how important it is for me and other preschool teachers to help prepare our young students for the rigors of academic life.

As a teacher of two- and three-year olds, I am often asked, "Why send a two-year old to preschool?" Well, if you look at the recent research on brain development, which states that the brain's foundations for all later learning are established in the first three years of life, it's easy to argue the benefits of sending a child as young as two to school.

Before birth, the prenatal brain creates the 100 billion neurons, or brain cells, that make up the brain. In the first few years of life, 700 neural connections, or synapses, between these brain cells are established every second, and each of these synapses contain bits of learned information.[20] Scientists have discovered that these synapses are affected by genetic makeup, the environment, and most importantly, by a child's early relationships with parents, teachers, and other caregivers. If these relationships, also referred to as "serve and return" relationships, are not nurturing and loving in nature and do not support the tremendous amount of learning that occurs in the first three years of life, the synapses could be disrupted. As a result, a child might child might suffer learning or behavioral disparities later in life that might be difficult to overcome.

Given the information we know about healthy brain development, it is clear that a loving, nurturing preschool program that encourages children to safely explore and learn in developmentally appropriate ways, will help a child establish a strong foundation for learning that will support more formal instruction later in life.

The four domains of child development are cognitive, language, movement, and social-emotional. The foundations for future learning in these four domains are established in infancy; however, there are other skills that cross all four domains. These skills, which are referred to as foundations of learning, or approaches to learning, are the way we use our brains for learning throughout our lives. Children are not born with these skills but are born with the ability to acquire them through relationships with loving, caring adults who support a child's ability to become a learner who is curious, focuses attention, remembers earlier experiences, gathers information, solves problems, and is persistent when challenged by a difficult task. As preschool teachers we have a responsibility to provide a learning environment that supports and encourages our students to develop these important skills so they can be successful in school and beyond.

CURIOSITY

Two-year olds are naturally curious individuals. In preschool, we strive to make our classrooms a place where our students can safely explore and learn. We provide a variety of toys and activities that encourage a child's

---

20 "In Brief: The Science of Early Childhood Development," Center on the Developing Child, Harvard University. http://www.developing child.harvard.edu.

natural curiosity and desire to explore the world around them. Children learn primarily through play, and as teachers, we can encourage curiosity in our students by making classroom materials easily accessible and by offering support without interfering with a child's natural curiosity. This curiosity is evident when we watch a student play with a classroom material such as Play-Doh. The child may squeeze and manipulate the Play-Doh or use tools to cut the Play-Doh into different shapes. They may continue to further explore the Play-Doh by touching and smelling it. The teacher may step in when they begin to explore the Play-Doh by trying to taste it.

MEMORY

When an infant or toddler uses memory to recall past information or experiences, it helps them to see the world as a familiar place so that they can begin to form a more intricate understanding of the world.[21] One way that preschool teachers could help students expand memory is by establishing classroom schedules and routines. In our classroom, we frequently model expected behaviors and prompt children to try to predict what comes next so that they can practice retrieving previously learned information and begin to commit that information to their long-term memory. For example, when it is time for snack, the children are expected to wash their hands before finding a place to sit at the table. Many of the children go right to the table when they see us getting ready for snack. Instead of telling them to go wash their hands, we might ask them, "What should we do before sitting down for snack?" In addition, frequent repetition of songs, rhymes, and stories also helps children expand their memory, not only of these familiar rhymes but also of information in general. Finger plays, songs, and rhymes are a main component of our daily meeting time in preschool.

ATTENTION

Focused attention is a fundamental element in cognitive development. It is well known that a toddler has a limited attention span, but there are developmentally appropriate methods that will help young children stay

21 Petersen, S. (2012). "School Readiness for Infants and Toddlers? Really? Yes, Really!", *Young Children*, 67(4), 10–13.

focused on a particular task or learning experience. In our classroom, we try and pay attention to a child's individual strengths and interests so that we may incorporate these interests into other areas of learning. For example, if a child loves to pretend to whip up meals in housekeeping, we might use that time to introduce colors, numbers, and sorting activities. As the child places food on the table, we might ask, "How many cookies are on this plate?" or "What color is this apple?" Taking advantage of these teachable moments, while the student is engaged in a favorite activity, may extend the amount of time they stay focused on the task.

INFORMATION GATHERING

Young children use observation and their senses to gather and process information. The way young children learn new information is through independent play and meaningful interactions with caring adults.[22] Preschool teachers encourage their young students to learn new information through exploration and play while also interacting with them using meaningful language to describe feelings, objects, and actions. An example of this kind of interaction might be when a student is playing with a magnetic toy. The teacher sitting nearby says, "You are playing with magnets. What happens when you put them together?" After the child puts them together, the teacher responds by saying, "Look, they stick together!" By interacting with the student and using meaningful language, the teacher has expanded the child's learning experience.

PROBLEM SOLVING

Children learn a tremendous amount of information in the first three years of life, and they encounter many challenges along the way. While it's not always easy, it is important to give children the freedom to try to find a solution on their own before stepping in and solving the problem for them. In the preschool classroom, we witness many instances where a child is faced with a problem, particularly when they are participating in play with another child. For instance, when a child has a toy taken away from them by another child, it is tempting to step in and give the toy back, but it is actually more advantageous if the teacher observes from a distance so that the child may have the opportunity to find an appropriate

---

22 Ibid.

solution on their own. If the child does need help, the teacher steps in and gives just enough assistance so that the child can move on to the next step in trying to solve the problem. Encouraging children to solve their own problems helps to build independence and feelings of self-confidence that will assist them in tackling challenging academic problems later in life.

PERSISTENCE THROUGH FRUSTRATION

Trying to persist through the many challenges presented in the first three years of life can certainly cause some feelings of frustration in a toddler. Many do not yet possess the ability to manage their feelings when faced with a challenge and give up before completing the task. Preschool teachers must gage a child's ability to regulate their feelings and provide appropriate activities that challenge a child without causing feelings of frustration. This is evident on the playground when a child attempts to climb a challenging structure or in the classroom when a student attempts to complete a puzzle. Teachers should always be available to offer words of encouragement to limit feelings of frustration and to help the child persevere and complete the challenging task.

Since brain research tells us that the foundation for all learning is set in the first three years of a child's life, a preschool teacher must play a vital role in the development of a healthy, well-constructed brain that is able to successfully navigate the challenges of academic life. It is imperative that preschool teachers establish loving, nurturing relationships with their students so that they can learn the appropriate social and emotional skills, such as curiosity, memory, focused attention, information gathering, problem solving, and persistence through frustration, that are necessary for a child's future academic success. They must also offer a safe environment with developmentally appropriate activities and experiences that encourage their students to learn and grow.

Preschool teachers should embrace the important role they play in helping to develop school readiness and academic success in a young child's life. I know I do!

Margy Hemmig teaches preschool at St. Andrew's.

Let Them Play (Part 1)

Play is critical to the social, emotional, and intellectual development of every child. When children play, they are engaged in the "purest expression of their humanity, the truest expression of their individuality."[23] Roam the halls and playgrounds of St. Andrew's lower school and realize that when you see children together creating and imagining, they are not just playing, they are learning.

At a time when so many school are reducing opportunities for play and recess, St. Andrew's is doing just the opposite for its preschool through third-grade students. Play is an integral part of the curriculum because we have intuitively known for years that play sparks learning.

Now research supports that intuition.

When we talk about play, we are describing those moments when the control of learning transfers from the teacher to the students. When children are role-playing different occupations or playing games to help their numeracy, the children's interactions, language, and thinking are being observed by the teacher. Playtime is safe, yet unstructured time, in which students get to develop both their intellectual quotient (IQ) but more importantly, what Daniel Goleman calls their emotional quotient (EQ).

"Let's Play!" are magic words when a young child hears them. To a child, it says: "You are fun," "You are my friend," "You are interested in me," and "I like you." Play promotes key 21st-century skills, including collaboration, critical thinking, and problem solving.

---

23   Brown, S. (2010) *Play: How It Shapes the Brain, Opens the Imagination, and Invigorates the Soul.* Avery Trade.

Ask any parent and they will agree that children need to play. Few adults would disagree that when we are at play is when our brains are most alive. "Neuroscientists and developmental psychologists, from every point of the compass know that play is a profound biological process... and lies at the core of creativity and innovation."[24]

Research by Gwen Dewar, PhD, found that play and exploration trigger the secretion of brain-derived neurotrophic factor, or BDNF, a substance that is essential for the growth of brain cells. Her studies show that play opportunities improve memory and stimulate the growth of the cerebral cortex. Several studies revealed that children pay more attention to academics after they have had recess. When playing, their interest is self-directed, and they are motivated to solve problems from the social and physical world that are important to them. Imagination and social play also supports the development of attention, self-control, and cooperative-learning skills.

From our observations as preschool and third-grade teachers, the benefits of play are many.

When children play, they are more concerned with the process than the product. They experiment and become more flexible in thinking and problem solving. When children play, they free themselves from external rules and may generate rules of their own, many times leading them to negotiation.

When children play, their own unique learning profile is developed and valued. One of the best ways for children to express themselves is through creative play. Play is vital to learning, as shown in the research of Kathy Hirsh-Pasek.[25] In observing pre-K children while building a bridge with blocks, they were engaged, paying attention, and controlling themselves as they collaborated, thus developing their focus and self-control. As they used blocks to represent a truck or car, they created symbolic representations, thus developing their ability to make cognitive

---

24   Ibid., 4–5.
25   See: Kathy Hirsh-Pasek's research (https://liberalarts.temple.edu/academics/faculty/ hirsh-pasek-kathryn); and Bartlett, T. (2011). "The Case for Play: How a Handful of Researchers Are Trying to Save Childhood," 20 February, *Chronicle of Higher Education*, http://chronicle.com/article/The-Case-for-Play/126382/.

connections. When the bridge fell down, they needed to rebuild it so it would not collapse, thus developing their critical thinking and resiliency.

According to Stuart Brown, the founder of National Institute for Play (www.nifplay.org), play is the child's way of coming to terms with personal experiences in, and knowledge of, the world.[26] Researchers, such as Daniel Willingham, acknowledge that when children become emotionally connected to learning events, such as play, it is beneficial to memory.[27]

So, what does play look like at St. Andrew's?

Play is integral in all aspects of early education. In the Responsive Classroom© (RC) setting, educators strive to meet student's need for a sense of belonging, significance, and fun—the guiding principles of the program. Inside the classroom, elementary-aged children find the fun in academic choice and game playing.

In parallel, outside play at recess and break time also cultivates a child's desire for free choice, personal responsibility and relationship building. Educational theorist Lev Vygotsky developed the "zone of proximal development," a level of cognitive development that is influenced by adults and other children's interactions with a specific child. According to Vygotsky, "In play the child always behaves beyond his average age, above his daily behavior; in play it is as though he were a head taller than himself. As in the focus of magnifying glass, play contains all developmental tendencies in a condensed form and is a major source of development."[28]

Vygotsky followers believe that a child's developmental growth is directly influenced by those around him or her. Educators are seen more as facilitators, and the greatest growth comes from the "give and take" of

---

26 Willingham, D. (2009). *Why Don't Student's Like School? A Cognitive Scientist Answers Questions about How the Mind Works and What It Means for the Classroom.* Jossey-Bass, 58.

27 Brown, S. and Vaughan, C. (2010). *Play: How It Shapes the Brain, Opens the Imagination, and Invigorates the Soul.* Penguin, 5.

28 Vygotsky, L. S. (1978). *Mind in Society: The Development of Higher Mental Processes.* Harvard University Press, 101. See also: Leon, D. and Bodrova, E. (2006). *Tools of the Mind: The Vygotskian Approach to Early Childhood Education.* Pearson.

everyday academic and social interactions with peers. Student's views and abilities are stretched from observing, copying, and integrating the social, emotional, and academic skills of their classmates.

When you ask a typical elementary-aged student his or her favorite part of the day, often the answer is "lunch" or "recess." While many educators may lament that response, the response actually highlights the paramount importance of unstructured time and play in a child's day.

So, as educators, and for you as the reader, what does this all mean?

What it means for us is a desire to "get out of your child's way," so children can play with ideas as well as each other. At St. Andrew's we offer choice in academics, to allow children a chance to play and have fun. We also recognize that homework should be limited so that your child can rest, regroup, and get ready to tackle the social, emotional, and academic work planned for the next day.

But only after they played their hearts out at home.

Peggy Best, who has since retired, taught pre-kindergarten and was Preschool Curriculum Coordinator during her writing of this research-informed story.

Dale Kynoch teaches third grade and was the Elementary Curriculum Coordinator.

Let Them Play (Part 2)

Physical education, what many readers might fondly remember as "gym," has changed. It's no longer about elimination games like dodgeball or conditioning exercises such as sit-ups, pushups, and pull-ups. P.E. is about developing competency in a variety of movement experiences. For instance, each year I strive to take my students on a P.E. field trip to the bowling alley. Before that, we were learning the volleyball bump using balloons, perfecting our downward dog position in yoga, playing Bocce in our underhand throwing unit, and learning the art of chasing, fleeing, and dodging through tagging games. We all know what happens when kids find something they love and that makes them feel good. Play and movement are dopamine-producing activities, and when children find something that they love, nothing else matters in their world. P.E. can help children discover a love of movement.

Unfortunately, not too many schools have chosen to let students play. The thinking is that to raise reading and math scores, students should be spending more time in those classes. Time is the prize in schools, and too often what gets cut is physical education and the arts. This choice runs counter to research in Mind, Brain and Education science.

From the perspective of learning, the research is clear that physical activity, as well as social support, are the two most important factors in reducing stress.[29] When you exercise, you turn on the front part of the brain where the prefrontal cortex, which plays a major role in executive

---

29 Cohen, S. and Ashby Wills, T. (1985). "Stress, Social Support and the Buffering Hypothesis." *Psychological Bulletin*, 98. See also: Rimmele, U., et al. (2009). "The Level of Physical Activity Affects Adrenal and Cardiovascular Reactivity to Psychosocial Stress." *Psychoneuroendocrinology* 34, 190–198.

function, resides. We know stress will manifest itself in the lives of every student, whether it is self-imposed or it comes from parents, teachers, or one's peers. But providing students strategies to deal with stress throughout their lives is critical to their emotional well-being. As Plato said so clearly to Hippocrates: "If you are in a bad mood, go for a walk. If you are still in a bad mood, go for another walk."

If you've read John Ratey's *Spark: The Revolutionary New Science of Exercise and the Brain*, then you already know and understand the benefits of movement and exercise on the brain. If you read the last issue of *Think Differently and Deeply*, then you know the benefits of play, especially unstructured play, in learning. We also know that unless kids start moving more, putting down their PlayStation and Xbox, this country will have an obesity epidemic. We hear it every time the argument for and against P.E. in schools gets started. Americans, both adults and children, are reaching epidemic levels of obesity, and schools play a critical role in developing a mindset of motion.[30]

Physical education and play also correlate to better academic outcomes and a drop in discipline problems. We have known for years that the fitter you are the better student you are.[31] If you want proof, look to Sweden where better aerobic capacity was shown to lead to an increased IQ.[32] Finally, it has been shown that movement and P.E. lower the internal state of noise and chaos for struggling students.[33]

But the argument to keep P.E. in schools isn't based solely on the benefits to the brain. It's because the research tells us that children who receive limited exposure to movement activities have fewer options later in life. Just as we teach math, language, arts, and science to prepare students to be competent

---

30 See: The Aspen Institute's Project Play report "Physical Literacy in the United States."

31 Ratey, J. J. and Hagerman, E. (2008). *Spark: The Revolutionary New Science of Exercise and the Brain (1st edition)*. Little, Brown and Company.

32 Åberg, M. A. I., Pedersen, N. L., Torén, K., Svartengren, M., Bäckstrand, B., Johnsson, T., Cooper-Kuhn, C. M., Åberg, N. D., Nilsson, M. and Kuhn, H. G. (2009). "Cardiovascular Fitness Is Associated with Cognition in Young Adulthood." *Proceedings of the National Academy of Sciences*, 106(49), 20906–11.

33 Pontifex, M. B., Saliba, B. J., Raine, L. B., Picchietti, D. L. and Hillman, C. H. (2013). "Exercise Improves Behavioral, Neurocognitive, and Scholastic Performance in Children with Attention-Deficit/Hyperactivity Disorder." *The Journal of Pediatrics*, 162(3), 543–51.

and capable adults, we also want our children to grow up to be happy and healthy adults. Therefore, we also need to give them the tools to manage both their stress and their overall health. The long-term goals of physical education teachers are not too distinct from teachers of other disciplines. For example, one of the hopes of a language arts teacher is to make each student a confident, independent, lifelong reader. For P.E. teachers, we want each student to become confident, independent lifelong movers.

So, the question should not be why do we need to keep physical education in schools, but rather why is it not as much a priority in schools as every other academic discipline. From my observations, I can tell you this: the disparity between children who have been engaged in and regularly receive developmentally appropriate, regular, and enriching movement experiences and those who do not is evident before they even get to kindergarten.

For those parents trying to turn their budding youth into a collegiate athlete by specializing in one sport, P.E. is about exposure to many options. Children who have only experienced a youth soccer league will lag behind their peers in throwing, catching, and striking skills, skills that are not explored on the soccer field. And when soccer is the only option for those children, they do not feel confident in joining in on the baseball game, or the gymnastics routines, or the yoga class that their peers are confidently enjoying.

In order for children to feel confident in any activity, they need exposure, education, and practice with the skills essential for successful participation. The best place to receive this instruction is in a P.E. class taught by an educator who understands how children learn and can patiently address each student's current neuromotor strengths and areas of challenge.

This is where it is important to understand the brain's wiring and the process of myelination. When my preschool through second-grade students are learning a new skill, whether it is to throw or kick a ball, catch, or run, learning the proper technique from the beginning is critical. As we know from brain plasticity, it is possible to rewire the brain. But when we initially learn a technique wrong, it will require building a new neural pathway to correct the flaw.

Children at St. Andrew's receive an average of 1.5 hours of instruction per week in movement education or physical education in grades preschool through second grade and 3 hours per week in grades 3–5. This is on top of their daily recess that they receive for an average of 45 minutes a day. By instilling this competency and a love of movement in children at a young age, they will seek out physical activity outside of school, at recess, on the playground, and as adults. It is no different than research on adult vocabulary and how it correlates to the amount of words a child was exposed to early in life. Children that feel capable and confident in a variety of movement experiences turn into adults that incorporate exercise into their daily lives because they enjoy it and have a variety of physical activities that they feel competent in doing.

The role of the P.E. teacher is to develop a joy of movement, and that comes when students develop competency in a variety of movement activities. This alone is why P.E. should be considered a central part of a school's program, and the fact that P.E. correlates to enhanced academic success, is merely, dare I say, game changing.

Nicole Starace teaches lower school physical education at St. Andrew's.

Mindfulness in the Lower School: Changing Brains One Breath at a Time

On an overcast and humid morning in March, I sat, eyes closed, my heart filled to the brim in the middle of the assembly hall, surrounded by silence, a calm energy filling the room. As I listened carefully, I could hear a pin drop, yet the students were not yet on Spring Break, and school was still in session. When I opened my eyes and looked around the auditorium, I saw the little chests of 80 preschool and elementary students rising and falling as they lay motionless on mats, backs flat on the ground, bellies filling with breath and exhaling. In the distance, a bell gently rang, bringing 80 pairs of eyes to attention and concluding the community Shavasana and our first lower school assembly.

This moment marked the end of a year-long exploration of the use of mindfulness and yoga practice in the classroom setting. The moment I looked around and made eye contact with the other adults in the room, including teachers, parents, family members, and significant others, I knew that this work had powerful, positive implications for both community engagement and the learning environment.

Two years earlier while on summer break I read *Wherever You Go There You Are* by Jon Kabat-Zinn, PhD, on the suggestion of a colleague, in hopes of finding some strategies for coping with pressures of a new leadership position while balancing the demands of raising a young family. I admit I was ambivalent at first about establishing a personal practice of mindfulness, but within a few weeks, I was beginning to make time and space for this daily discipline.

These experiences led me to explore other books on the subject, specifically related to the implementation of mindfulness in the classroom. As a school administrator, I was in search of an approach to teaching and learning that balanced the external processing necessary for social and emotional learning (SEL) while acknowledging and understanding the forces of emotion that so often derailed these formal structures when working with young children.[34]

The more I read on the subject of mindfulness, the more I learned about the potential benefits, from increased attention and enhanced emotional regulation to greater self-regulation and overall improvement in health and well-being. Preliminary studies of mindfulness have underscored the positive impact on physical, social, and psychological well-being and potential improvements in academic performance, suggesting practitioners can reduce levels of cortisol, the hormone most closely associated with stress, and experience increased optimism and executive function skills.[35, 36, 37]

The most exciting aspect this work for me was the positive impact of mindfulness experienced not only by students, but also by teachers. The teaching profession is one of great responsibility and intense pressure as demands and constraints continually increase and rewards remain meager. Across the profession, absenteeism and health-related productivity issues result in teacher burnout, and ultimately good teachers with great intentions leave the profession.

---

34 When educating the whole child, the importance of SEL is at the heart of the learning experience. At St. Andrew's Episcopal School, we have known about the importance of scaffolding SEL into all aspects of the learning experience and have implemented the Responsive Classroom curriculum as a formal way to teach SEL.

35 Gallant, S. N. (2016) "Mindfulness Meditation Practice and Executive Functioning: Breaking down the Benefit," *Consciousness and Cognition*, 40 (February), 116–30.

36 Tang, Y.-Y., Ma, Y., Wang, J., Feng, S., Lu, Q., Yu, Q., Sui, D., Rothbart, M. K., Fan, M. and Posner, M. I. (2007). "Short-Term Meditation Training Improves Attention and Self-Regulation", *PNAS Journal*, 104(43), 17152–6.

37 Gritz, J. R. (2015). "Mantras before Math Class," *The Atlantic*, November 10.

Exceptional teachers are not immune to exhaustion and are at an even greater risk given their high degree of perfectionism. At St. Andrew's we have many master teachers, like skillful scientists and expert artists. They balance both the science and the art of the profession to create the most favorable learning conditions for students to thrive. Recent research has highlighted the benefits of mindfulness-based stress reduction for teachers, citing improved self-compassion and sleep habits, increased working memory, and lower levels of occupational stress.[38]

Imagine for a second that two students of any age are squabbling in the classroom—over the desired seat, or access to shared materials, or about a mutual friend. Progressively each child becomes more frustrated and overwhelmed by emotion. Unable to cope, one or both of the children act impulsively—possibly aggressively—with words or actions that hurt one another. As a teacher or parent in the situation, we aim to educate and seek reparations when necessary, often repeating: "Say you're sorry," "Calm down," or my favorite: "Listen."

How often have we seen or found ourselves in this exact situation? It is incredible how we as adults react when we become stressed. An overused but useful metaphor helps illustrate the importance of self-care for teachers: you must put your breathing mask on yourself before you can help those around you. As a result of my personal mindfulness practice, it became clear to me that the first step on this journey was to empower the teachers.

Initially, the goal was to provide multiple opportunities for teachers to explore mindfulness to develop a personal practice. Much the same way I had come to value the importance of mindfulness in my own life, I wanted my colleagues to experience the same results. My instincts told me that a master teacher is also a mindful teacher, who navigates these everyday classroom distractions while honoring each child's perspective in a way that enhances the learning environment.

The first year of our journey focused on helping teachers to experience mindfulness in their own lives and encouraging them to harness those

---

38   Flook, L., Goldberg, S. B., Pinger, L., Bonus, K. and Davidson, R. J. (2013). "Mindfulness for Teachers: A Pilot Study to Assess Effects On Stress, Burnout, and Teaching Efficacy." *Mind, Brain, and Education*, 7(3), 182–95.

tools and bring them to their classroom practice. As with any initiative, you have your early adopters and your skeptics. This work was not mandated, rather recommended—allowing teachers to have autonomy and time to develop a personal connection to mindfulness practice.

By year two, my lower school faculty was eager to implement mindfulness practices in the classroom. Local partnerships brought additional training in classroom strategies and helped to operationalize these practices for students. At St. Andrew's we preach that teachers are brain changers, and neuroscience was validating that mindfulness had the potential to change minds as well.

Harvard University unveiled an MRI study proving that meditation can produce massive changes in the brain's grey matter. Participants reported reductions in stress that correlated to a decrease in the density of grey matter in the amygdala, part of the brain known to play a significant role in anxiety and stress. These reductions also coincided with a major increase in grey matter in the hippocampus, the part of the brain associated with self-awareness, compassion, and introspection. Sara Lazar, the study's senior author and member of the Psychiatric Neuroimaging Research Program at Massachusetts General Hospital, reported the study "demonstrates that changes in the brain structure may underlie some of the improvements,"[39] indicating that mindfulness has the potential to change our brain structure and promote healthy learning behaviors such as increased optimism and inhibition.[40]

After several years of applying this approach as a teacher and as an administrator, I realized that developing a consistent practice of mindfulness provided structure and routine, essential components of a safe environment and a culture of caring. I observed students' enhanced emotional literacy and expanded perspective-taking skills as a result of this blended approach to social and emotional learning (SEL) that included elements of mindfulness and yoga practice. When children can self-regulate, they understand why they have a particular feeling and are better equipped to manage emotions, communicate needs, understand

39   McGreevey, S. (2011). "Eight Weeks to a Better Brain." *Harvard Gazette*.
40   Oberle, E., Schonert-Reichl, K. A., Lawlor, M. S. and Thomson, K. C. (2012). "Mindfulness and Inhibitory Control in Early Adolescence." *Journal of Early Adolescence*, 32(4), 565–88.

the perspective of others, and identify win-win situations.[41] Thus cultivating SEL and mindfulness in tandem integrates competencies such as self-awareness, relationship-building, and decision-making skills into a conflict resolution framework, empowering children both to be aware of their emotions and thoughts and to equip them with structures to regulate their behavior and make healthy choices. Linda Lantieri, Senior Program Advisor, Collaborative for Academic, Social, and Emotional Learning (CASEL), states that "mindfulness practices connect students' inner and outer experiences and help them to see the congruence between the two."[42] By the third year of our mindfulness journey, teachers noted anecdotally that students were more engaged and attentive following mindful moments in the classroom.

As we prepare to enter our fourth year of implementing mindfulness into all aspects of classroom learning, I remain optimistic about its impact on student learning and well-being. Research on this topic is still in the early stages but suggests the positive benefits of mindfulness for our students and teachers. While many of these studies focus on the impact of mindfulness in early adolescence and young adults, I continue to be interested in the effect of mindfulness on young children. Promoting these behaviors and deepening an understanding of these practices at a young age has the potential to improve health, happiness, and school achievement in later years.

I am excited to implement a curriculum this year that uses mindfulness practice as the foundation for each lesson, including topics such as conflict resolution, kindness, and empathy. I am also excited to be undertaking our own research to investigate the connection between blended SEL and mindfulness practices and student outcomes.

---

41   Borba, M. (2017). *Unselfie: Why Empathetic Kids Succeed in Our All-About-Me World*. Touchstone, 97.

42   Zakrzewski, V. and Lantieri, L. (2015). "How Social-Emotional Learning and Mindfulness Can Work Together." *Huffpost Education*, April 14.

Jordan Love is co-head of the lower school at St. Andrew's.

Planting Seeds of Kindness

One day this summer, I decided to dodge my rather dull "to-do" list, which included writing an essay for this volume of *Think Differently and Deeply*, and head to the local pool with my daughter. As I watched her practice flip turns, my mind flitted to ideas about how to approach writing this article. Then, an unexpected gift arrived.

A barefoot toddler padded over in my direction, stood in front of the chair next to me and reached down to pick up a brown hair tie from the ground. He looked up, handed it to me with a broad smile, and said, "Here!"

My heart nearly melted. This child gave me an object he thought I needed, with nothing to gain and no prompting from his father—who stood in the pool waiting to resume their game. The child's simple act of kindness came from a place deep inside, and I happened to be the lucky recipient.

A 2012 study suggests that kindness is intrinsically rewarding to young children. Toddlers appeared happier when they gave away a treat of their own to a puppet than when they received a treat for themselves.[43] Practicing kindness not only makes us feel good, it helps children strengthen peer relationships, increases prosocial behaviors (i.e., behaviors that benefit others or society as a whole), happiness, self-esteem, gratitude, and well-being.[44]

Research shows that children have a capacity for kindness, but also a capacity for cruelty that can rear its ugly head in a tendency to

43   Aknin, L. B., Hamlin, J. K. and Dunn, E. W. (2012). "Giving Leads to Happiness in Young Children." *PLoS ONE*, 7(6).
44   Borba, M. (2017). *UnSelfie: Why Empathetic Kids Succeed in Our All-About-Me World*. Touchstone.

exclude those unlike them in race, language, gender, social groups, and behaviors.[45, 46] These findings reveal an exciting window of opportunity to teach our youngest learners how to tip the balance of their scales in favor of kindness.

Our preschool teaching philosophy at St. Andrew's is anchored in our belief that teaching social-emotional skills—sharing, comforting, self-regulation, empathy, listening, and cooperation—provides the foundation for learning and success at school and beyond.

A 2015 study showed five-year-old students with higher prosocial skills were more likely to have more successful outcomes as adults in key areas such as education, employment, substance abuse, and mental health.[47] In addition, a large meta-analysis of 213 social-emotional learning programs indicated that students participating in them showed improvements in many areas, including social-emotional skills and academic achievement.[48]

How can we influence, strengthen, and extend our students' capacity for kindness? Laying our professional insights as teachers alongside insights from research suggests a direction to explore. It all starts with developing what's on the inside with these four approaches:

HELP BUILD EMOTIONAL AWARENESS

Preschool students express a broad range of emotions every day—some joyful, some not. When students experience a conflict or feel strong emotion, teachers provide verbal support and visual prompts to help children stop, take deep breaths, problem-solve, and move forward.

45 Licona, T. (2018). *How to Raise Kind Kids: And Get Respect, Gratitude, and a Happier Family in the Bargain.* Penguin Books.

46 Wittmer, D. S., Petersen, S. H. and Puckett, M. B. (2017). *The Young Child: Development from Prebirth through Age Eight.* Pearson.

47 Jones, D. E., Greenberg, M. and Crowley, M. (2015). "Early Social-Emotional Functioning and Public Health: The Relationship Between Kindergarten Social Competence and Future Wellness." *American Journal of Public Health*, 105(11), 2283–90.

48 Durlak, J. A., Weissberg, R. P., Dymnicki, A. B., Taylor, R. D. and Schellinger, K. B. (2011). "The Impact of Enhancing Students' Social and Emotional Learning: A Meta-Analysis of School-Based Universal Interventions: Social and Emotional Learning." *Child Development*, 82(1), 405–32.

Children use fun breathing strategies like bunny breathing to increase oxygen flow and improve their ability to think more clearly. With practice, children learn how to identify and talk about their feelings. Once our youngest students can name feelings in themselves, they are more likely to identify and relate to the feelings of others. Teaching kindness is not only possible, but achievable, when we increase emotional awareness.

PRACTICE WHAT YOU PREACH

If we want seeds of kindness to grow strong roots, teachers must model kindness for students in what we say, how we say it, and what we do. We offer comfort, love, and support to each child to meet their unique needs. Sometimes, a simple hug can change the trajectory of a child's day! As children feel safe, secure, and valued, their minds open up to engage in higher-order thinking. In keeping with our Responsive Classroom curriculum, we use positive teacher language and encourage a St. Andrew's "yet" mindset. Negative "I can't do it!" thinking is replaced with "maybe not yet...let's keep trying!" Modeling kindness doesn't stop with our students! Celebrate your co-teacher's birthday with the children, open a door for someone, greet colleagues with a smile, or give a compliment! We know children are more likely to practice kindness when they see it, hear it, and feel it all around them, all the time.

HIGHLIGHT THE POSITIVE

Noticing and naming prosocial behavior goes a long way in helping children understand what kindness means. "Joe feels better now that you brought him the toy he wanted. That was kind of you." The more we identify and encourage acts of kindness, children will be more likely to repeat them. A year ago, one of our students was stuck in a grumpy mood. "No!" was a word she knew all too well, until one of us discovered her shoes. "Wow! I notice you have different shoes today. They are pink and sparkly!" She smiled, and her mood switched—just, like, *that*! We realized she was seeking out a connection, a way to feel she was valued and known. Brain research tells us that emotion and cognition are intertwined.[49] If we

---

49   Okon-Singer, H., Hendler, T., Pessoa, L. and Shackman, A. J. (2015). "The Neurobiology of Emotion–Cognition Interactions: Fundamental Questions and Strategies for Future Research." *Frontiers in Human Neuroscience*, 9.

teach with intention, we can create meaningful experiences that generate positive emotions, paving the way for better learning.

COACH FOR CHARACTER

St. Andrew's is a place of learning that values the education of the spirit as well as the mind. We teach children the Golden Rule: treat others as you want to be treated. Teachers coach ethical behavior by role-playing scenarios with one another at circle, meeting time, or during play. We ask questions, listen to student feedback, and challenge students to think harder and deeper about feelings and choices. What could you do to make this person feel better? What other choice could you make? How did this book character make you feel?

St. Andrew's teachers understand the importance of planting seeds of kindness in early childhood. We not only help children develop their moral character, but also establish an intertwined system of roots so kindness can grow and blossom beyond our school walls.

Denise Kotek taught preschool at St. Andrew's during the writing of this research-informed article.

The Science of Reading: Transforming Our Approach to Reading Instruction from Good to Great for All Our Students

In the middle of a pandemic with no visible ending, the leadership in our elementary and early childhood divisions made the bold decision to fully align our instructional approach and curriculum with the growing body of research referred to as the "science of reading." I've always felt that being a teacher in our school is not for the faint of heart, but it could never be truer than this year.

WHEN YOU KNOW BETTER, DO BETTER

Within our faculty, we have a collective culture of striving to grow in our professional capacity as teachers. For us, this means taking action to become ever more aligned with the findings of emerging research. Over two years, several lower school faculty members and leaders took a deep dive into what is currently known about reading acquisition as part of the literature review process in the creation of "The Elementary Roadmap."[50] This is a resource we created for our own teachers, K–fifth grade, to curate important findings in mind, brain, and education (MBE) studies that

---

50   The Centre for Transformative Teaching & Learning. (no date). "The MBE Placemat and the Elementary Roadmap". www.thecttl.org/the-mbe-placemat-and-the-elementary-roadmap/.

speak directly to the elementary learning environment. What we found was compelling data on specific skills and instructional practices found to be essential for the ultimate goal of high-level reading comprehension for all. We had to act.

To start us off, the Simple View of Reading theory[51] was very helpful because it takes a whole ecosystem of reading processes and collects them under two overarching domains: word recognition and concepts of language. These include acquiring knowledge of the alphabetic system, learning to decode new words, building a vocabulary of words that can be read from memory by sight, and becoming facile at constructing, integrating, and remembering meanings represented in text.[52] The other body of research that guided our decisions showed strong evidence for the importance of a comprehensive, structured, explicit, and cumulative approach to teaching the concepts and skills of reading.[53]

MEASURING IMPACT FROM THE START

The very first thing to do was comprehensively assess a wide range of foundational reading skills in order to gain a better understanding of exactly what each student brought with them into the classroom. This required a paradigm shift in how we understood our students as readers. We had to move away from the idea that a reader's skill could be accurately represented by any one assessment, to utilizing a suite of assessments that provide a snapshot of how a student functions across the many skills shown to be essential for the development of reading comprehension. Taking this approach allowed us to create a profile of each reader and from that, build clear pathways forward to target specific areas of weakness and strength identified in the process. We also had to let go of thinking that advanced reading comprehension was an appropriate measure for an early elementary student, and trust that the skills we now focus on, including

---

51 Gough, P. and Turner, W. (1986). "Decoding, Reading, and Reading Disability." *Remedial and Special Education*, 7(1), 6–10.

52 Hua, A. and Keenan, J. (2017). "Interpreting Reading Comprehension Test Results: Quantile Regression Shows that Explanatory Factors Can Vary with Performance Level." *Scientific Studies of Reading*, 21, 1–14.

53 Ehri, L., Nunes, S., Stahl, A. and Willows, D. (2002). "Systematic Phonics Instruction Helps Students Learn to Read: Evidence from the National Reading Panel's Meta-Analysis." *Journal of Direct Instruction*, 2(2), 121–66.

phonemic awareness, phonics, orthographic mapping, and fluency, are the building blocks of reading comprehension and deserve to be assessed in their own right as we introduce and practice new concepts. This does not mean we stop actively cultivating the strategies and perspectives of comprehension, but rather understand that we are cultivating these at this early age with no expectation of mastery while the student continues to build fluency and develops as a human being with growing executive function and concept processing capacity.

Collecting this data as a division will allow us to map impact over time and use our own research to validate choices, tweak implementation, and re-address areas showing low impact to sustain this transformation and iterate our responses to the science of reading research with constant, gentle improvement as the goal.

SHARED TEACHER VOCABULARY FOR READING INSTRUCTION

Identifying the important pieces of the reading puzzle along with the pedagogy proven to positively impact outcomes was only the first step. We quickly realized that our habitual understanding of the vocabulary and concepts of reading were hindering our ability to fully implement our vision. As an example, we had to ask the questions: what exactly is *syntax*? What impacts the development of syntax awareness? How can I recognize issues with syntax? What are some strategies I can use with my class to improve comprehension using improved use of syntax? Through healthy debate and the use of reliable source materials,[54] we are currently unpacking long-held myths and building a common understanding within our faculty of the nuances for each foundational concept so important to our decision-making process.

TEACHING SYNTAX AT ALL GRADE LEVELS

Syntax is the structure, organization, and rhythm of words to create sentences and phrases. This is unique for every language and holds some markers of dialectic difference within a language. Example: "The big blue

---

54 Eunice Kennedy Shriver National Institute of Child Health and Human Development. (2000). *Report of the National Reading Panel: Teaching Children to Read* (00-4769). Washington, DC: US Government Printing Office.

ball rolled quickly down the hill," is an example of generally accepted syntax for American English. "Ball the blue big rolled the hill down quickly" uses all the same words but follows unconventional syntax, essentially creating ambiguity of meaning. Knowing the relationship between the subject and the predicate, or rules of adjective order, is essential for the clarification of meaningful sentences in a text. When reading, we apply our knowledge of these rules to support comprehension.

Syntax becomes increasingly complex as a student makes their way through school. At each level, teachers have a responsibility to explicitly teach the rules of syntax that govern the texts a student will encounter in that class. This is especially important in content areas with specific jargon and norms of information sharing. Students with reading comprehension challenges often read passively, having not yet built the saliency needed to recognize all the clues of meaning. Teaching our students to actively seek syntactic information as they read has a strong impact on reading outcomes.

Limitations in awareness of syntax can be evident when a reader knows all the words in a text, but falters or rereads often to get the correct phrasing intended by the author. This can sound as if the student is ignoring punctuation cues and running parts of sentences together. It can also be evident in writing when older students continue to construct simple sentences without the complexity you would expect for their age. Note: Children who get cochlear implants often need explicit instruction in the rules of syntax as an intervention for the reading challenges caused by hearing limitations while very young.

Direct instruction, fun activities constructing and combining sentences using manipulatives or visuals, and sentence frames are just a few strategies shown to improve syntax use and awareness while reading and writing. In fact, writing can be a direct pathway to improved syntax awareness while reading when combined with explicit instruction, modeled examples, and a feedback loop targeting progress with the use of syntax in student writing.

We continue to adjust our reading curriculum and instructional approach invigorated by the stories of newfound success reported by families, observed by teachers, and felt among students. Empowering children to become self-directed analysts of the reading code and explicitly linking their knowledge of spoken (or signed) language to their knowledge of written language[55] is laying the foundation for a slow revolution toward a school culture bathed in literacy. Skilful effort lingers joyfully.

Christine Lewis was the lower school Learning Strategist at St. Andrew's and CTTL lower school Research-Lead during the writing of this research-informed article.

---

55 Ehri, L., Nunes, S., Stahl, A. and Willows, D. (2002). "Systematic Phonics Instruction Helps Students Learn to Read: Evidence from the National Reading Panel's Meta-Analysis." *Journal of Direct Instruction*, 2(2), 121–66.

The Connected and Valued Child

Feeling valued socially. Feeling emotionally connected. A student who experiences both those feelings is better able to use his or her whole mind to maximize learning potential. That raises one very important question: How does your child's school care for his or her social and emotional needs? The Responsive Classroom approach to teaching and learning is used at St. Andrew's from preschool through sixth grade, and it has transformed how students feel about themselves as individuals and as members of our community.

Several years ago, a father of one of my students made it clear to me that the only thing he cared about was his child's academic standing. He put no stock in whether his child had any friends or could function as a contributing member of the class. At the time, I had only recently been introduced to the Responsive Classroom approach[56] and while I believed on an intuitive level that academic and social success are interconnected, I was not able to articulate the research that supported the important role social and emotional skills played in the ongoing academic success of a developing child.[57] What I would have directed this parent to is the Responsive Classroom Efficacy Study that shows when the Responsive Classroom is "faithfully implemented, the approach correlated with a substantial rise-a roughly 20-point gain on average-on state standardized test scores in reading and math.[58]

---

56   Rimm-Kaufman, S. and Sawyer, B. (2012). "Efficacy of the Responsive Classroom Approach: Results from a Three Year, Longitudinal Randomized Control Trial."

57   Hinshaw, S. (1992). "Externalizing Behavior Problems and Academic Underachievement in Childhood and Adolescence: Causal Relationships and Underlying Mechanisms." *Psychological Bulletin,* 111, 127–55.

58   Mosle, S. (2012). "Teaching Lessons," *The New York Times Opinion Pages,* 27 October.

Many years later, I often think of that conversation and wish that I could have the opportunity to share with that father the clarity I have obtained, through experience and study, in this important area of teaching and learning.

Responsive teaching practices are built on the fundamental belief that along with a child's need for shelter, food, sleep, and familial love, each growing person is also driven by the need to belong, to feel that their presence is important, and to participate in playful, engaging experiences.[59] Responsive teachers also believe that social skills are like any of the other content areas, such as reading, math, and the arts, and as such, need to be explicitly taught, learned, and practiced for children to reach their full potential.

Walking into a responsive classroom on any given day, you will see the direct effect of these central principles in a myriad of ways. From the teacher's choice of words, to active modeling of expectations, to collaborative grouping, to options for academic choice, and the obviously student-owned approach to classroom rules of conduct.[60]

Responsive teachers begin each day with a community meeting with the intention of developing a strong sense of belonging and significance. This is accomplished by ensuring that every student's voice is heard and honored within the first few moments of each school day through opportunities to share his or her ideas and experiences with their learning community.

Perhaps one of the most tangible outcomes from this approach came during the 2011–2012 school year when our fourth-grade class had a difficult mid-year change; twins who had both been key members of our classroom community were moving away. You might be asking, "How would such a move impact the learning environment for the students who remained in the class?"

Using the routine of sharing in our morning meeting, children talked about their wishes for the twins in such a way that both the twins and their classmates felt better about the change. The structure of sharing

---

59   Kriete, R. (2002). *The Morning Meeting Book: Strategies for Teachers Series.* Northeast Foundation for Children, 9.

60   Charney, R. (2002). *Teaching Children to Care.* Northeast Foundation for Children, 17–36.

allowed children to find connections with others while sharing things that concerned them. This is not something that fourth-graders would typically feel comfortable doing!

Another central purpose of our social and emotional curriculum is the creation of self-regulation in children. Establishing a democratic classroom that addresses the developmental social and emotional needs of our students is fundamental to the Responsive Classroom CARES approach. Cooperation, Assertion, Responsibility, Empathy, and Self-Regulation are the core qualities that we actively seek to nurture within our students every day of school. It is truly inspiring to observe our children offer an authentic apology of action in a clear, calm, and empathetic manner after having discussed the impact of hurtful actions and brainstormed ways we can fix someone's hurt feelings. These human skills may seem far removed from the execution of algebra; however, in order to achieve the complicated abstract mental processes necessary for success in math, or indeed any academic discipline, a growing child requires healthy social connection, a belief that their presence matters, and confidence in their own ability to manage the emotional ups and downs that we all experience when exploring new territory.[61]

Reflection is also a key element in a responsive classroom; the end of each day is celebrated with a short community gathering where we actively think back over our day together. These moments of acknowledgment have a profoundly positive influence to support our children in their efforts to understand their own strengths and challenges as learners. It also serves to reinforce strategies for regulating their own behavioral responses. A favorite of mine is the "Compliment Circle,"[62] where students randomly take a card saying "You helped someone today" or "You took a learning risk today" and choose someone within their class to give it to. I saw the power of this activity in the life of a child who worked daily on impulse control challenges when a classmate gave him a card that said "You showed kindness today." The child receiving the card was so taken aback by a classmate noticing his kind act that he began to view

61   Graviano, P., et al. (2007). "The Role of Emotion Regulation and Children's Early Academic Success." Journal of School Psychology, 45, 3–19.
62   Januszka, D. and Vincent, K. (2012). Closing Circles: 50 Activities for Ending the Day in a Positive Way. Northeast Foundation for Children, 40.

himself differently and found new motivation to redirect his energy in positive ways. The results were not short-lived but continued to fuel his efforts toward self-control throughout the year. This is valuable work not only for the well-being of our students, but also because we know that the ability to exercise self-control is a strong predictor of academic success.[63]

The Responsive Classroom approach reaches far beyond the old perception of social and emotional curriculums producing "nice" kids in a warm and fuzzy environment. It allows us to build intelligent guidelines for school and to develop classroom practices that are informed by current neuroscience[64] and are relevant to the children of the 21st century.

The teachers and administration at St. Andrew's understand the importance of social cognition as integral to the process of learning for every child. The commitment to this truth has enriched the relationships within the faculty, powered the direction of administrative decisions, and led to happy, self-directing children, who relish their academic successes and believe in their ability to overcome their academic challenges.

Natalie Adams was head of the Intermediate School and Christine Lewis was a first-grade teacher and a Responsive Classroom® facilitator at St. Andrew's during the writing of this research-informed article.

Many of us Responsive Classroom believers have known for years that children are happy and successful when they participate in classrooms using Responsive Classroom; classrooms with daily Morning Meetings, Academic Choice, and teachers who use conscious and careful Teacher Language. Now there is data to support these observations.

For the past three years, Professor Sara Rimm Kaufman from the University of Virginia's Curry School of Education has been studying the efficacy of Responsive Classroom. The research focused on a correlation between the Responsive Classroom programs' impact on student-teacher

---

63   Shoda, Y. Mischel, W. and Peake, P. L. (1990) "Predicting Adolescent Cognitive and Self-Regulatory Competencies from Preschool Delay of Gratification: Identifying Diagnostic Conditions." *Developmental Psychology*, 26(26), 978–86.

64   Walsh, D. (March 2012). The Brain Goes to School. Educating the Whole Child: Learning and the Brain Society Conference.

interactions as well as math test gains. This study, which found that "frequent use of the approach's strategies was correlated with higher math achievement"[65] gave us data that confidently supports the link between academic and social-emotional learning.

When I first learned about Professor Rimm Kaufman's study, one of the parts that I found the most intriguing is how she evaluated the degree to which Responsive Classroom practices were used within schools and classrooms. After talking with her at a conference, Professor Rimm Kaufman shared with me the survey manual that she used to measure fidelity to the Responsive Classroom approach.

One major focus of the survey, and one I really love, is how it encourages teachers to self-evaluate and incorporate that self-reflection, along with classroom observation, to measure teacher's use of Responsive Classroom. I am planning this year to bring in elements of the study for my own observation and evaluation of our teachers in the Intermediate School division.

Since St. Andrew's Episcopal School values reflection in conjunction with observation, these new measures are a natural extension of the work that we already do. In my mind, this is a case of research informing practice in the most fluid and natural way.

---

65 Rimm-Kaufman, S. and Sawyer, B. (2012). "Efficacy of the Responsive Classroom Approach: Results from a Three Year, Longitudinal Randomized Control Trial." See also: Hinshaw, S. (1992). "Externalizing Behavior Problems and Academic Underachievement in Childhood and Adolescence: Causal Relationships and Underlying Mechanisms." *Psychological Bulletin*, 111, 127-55. See also: Kriete, R. (2002). *The Morning Meeting Book: Strategies for Teachers Series*. Northeast Foundation for Children, 9.

Teachers' Pets

Of the many educational tools commonly found in preschool classrooms, I have come to believe strongly through my experience as an early childhood educator that there is something truly special about classroom pets, something that can only be taught by a living, breathing thing.

Preschool classroom staples such as Play-Doh, train sets, Lego sets, puzzles, and building blocks help teach our children a host of valuable lessons from sharing to mathematics. They engage their imaginations and spark their creativity. These are all wonderful educational tools that I have used to great effect throughout my career.

The simple classroom pet, however, is perhaps the one common classroom item that teaches young children perhaps the most important lesson of all: empathy.

Why do I place empathy so high among the many learned human capacities? I believe that from empathy stems many of our most noble character traits. Kindness, understanding, generosity, gentleness, patience, and politeness all result from our ability to understand, share the feelings of, and relate to the many living beings for whom we care and with whom we interact. For children especially, classroom pets are effective teachers of empathy simply because so many young people happen to naturally love animals. Thus, by engaging their instincts to play with, pet, hold, and speak to animals, they begin to empathize with their smaller, more vulnerable friends without even realizing it. While to them they are having fun with a fluffy little friend, to us they are building character.

Classroom pets (in our case, two adorable guinea pigs named Pumpkin and YoYo) are also valuable in teaching young children about basic responsibility and the payoff in confidence and self-assurance that fulfilling one's responsibilities provides. We have several classroom "jobs" that my students rotate through on a weekly basis, and without fail those pertaining to the guinea pigs are the most popular. So once again without even realizing it, my students benefit from the presence of our wonderful little classroom pets by learning to be responsible for creatures that genuinely need them.

This point is well-stated in a 2015 article by Pets in the Classroom[66] a grant program that provides funding to pre-K through eighth grade teachers for the purpose of purchasing and maintaining classroom pets:

> When small pets are part of the classroom experience, students are benefitting. Numerous studies show the positive impact pets can have on kids, and teachers are seeing this impact in the classroom as well. Students are not only more excited about learning, they are also developing empathy and compassion by becoming aware of the needs of these animals and by seeing how their actions affect their little friends.

It is also important to note that not only do classroom pets help build a child's capacity for empathy, compassion, and responsibility for perhaps the first time in their young lives, but they even have the power to reverse certain negative learned behaviors that may have been developed prior to entering preschool, kindergarten, or early elementary school.

From the same Pets in the Classroom report, a Fort Worth, TX, teacher observed:

> "My students come from very poor, rough neighborhoods and homes. When school first started six weeks ago, I had to write multiple referrals per day for violent acts. Since Ella the Guinea Pig came to share our classroom, I have not had any violent acts and the noise level has gone way down because they don't want her to be frightened. They beg their families to let them bring a carrot stick from home or they ask me if

---

66 American Humane Association (July 2015). "Pets in the Classroom Study: Phase 1 Findings Report." https://www.americanhumane.org/app/uploads/2016/08/PETS-IN-THE-CLASSROOM-CKT-R4.pdf.

they can save part of their lunch to share with her. The best part is watching the empathy they developed for Ella begin to transfer to their peers. Ella has done something in four weeks that I may or may not have been able to do all year."

Though I have been lucky not to have to deal with violence among my students, I have seen on many occasions children saving bits of their own lunches to bring back to Pumpkin and YoYo. What a lovely gesture! A young (and presumably hungry!) child sacrificing a bit of their own lunch in order to do something special for their little friends back in the classroom is a remarkable act of selflessness, especially coming from a four-year-old!

I believe it is impulses such as these that, if continually encouraged and nurtured, will help our children grow into kind, compassionate, happy, and healthy adults. Our youth are our most precious asset, and we owe them such lessons. Thankfully, something so simple as providing them with pets in the classroom can help pave the way for such goals to be achieved.

Kristin Bartlett taught preschool at St. Andrew's during the writing of this research-informed article.

The Differentiated Classroom

Some years ago, a student new to St. Andrew's told me he did not like math and was not interested in learning any that year. Over the next few weeks, I taught and observed this student in the classroom and on the playground. He was a bright child, quick to understand new concepts, but had little background knowledge. He was missing essential knowledge and skills in many areas, including math, which dampened his enthusiasm for learning. To help him find success in the classroom, I spent a large part of the year identifying these gaps of knowledge and filling them in so he could gain confidence and have a solid foundational knowledge base that would allow him to progress successfully with his class.

A differentiated classroom is one in which teachers place great focus on who they are teaching, in addition to the subject matter that is being taught. It is an idea supported by research that shows that students' learning is enhanced when lessons are planned taking into account their differences. At St. Andrew's, a differentiated classroom means that teachers understand that students will come to them with varying levels of knowledge and skills and accept it as their professional responsibility to meet students where they are, engaging and appropriately challenging them to maximize their learning. We do this with the understanding that differences can stem from a myriad of origins. They can be due to socio-economic, cultural, racial, or gender factors, as well as because of individual learning differences, readiness, or personal affinities. All these elements can cause a group of students to enter our classrooms at the beginning of each school year with a collection of knowledge and skills that spans far beyond a developmental year.

To teach our students while being mindful of their differences, we need to know how these factors have shaped who they are. In this way, differentiating begins with knowing the student. St. Andrew's mission statement, "to know and inspire each child in an inclusive community dedicated to exceptional teaching, learning and service," reflects our dedication to differentiation.

Differentiation is predicated on knowing the child, knowing what their interests are, what values are taught at home, customs that they are familiar and not so familiar with, their current neurodevelopmental strengths and weaknesses, emotional and social maturity, as well as prior knowledge upon which curricular content will be built upon. Differences in the classroom can be vast. I remember a six-year-old student whose knowledge of the world was limited and who could not even tell me her last name, while another could tell me accurate historical details about the city of Pompeii. Some students struggle with adding single-digit numbers, while others are successfully adding two-digit numbers up to one hundred. A student who is academically capable may find it challenging to work with a partner, while another student seems to have the capacity to make every partnership a success.

From the moment a student first walks into our classroom, teachers seek to understand these differences that make each child unique. We interact with and observe the child in academic and non-academic settings, noting how she or he accomplishes specific tasks, problem solves, deals with frustration, and interacts with peers and adults. We also use formative assessments that tell us where the student is in terms of specific academic skills. Over time, the data we collect will allow a pattern to emerge highlighting the student's current neurodevelopmental strengths and challenges that have to do with learning.

We consider this information together with what we know about the student's emotional profile, and readiness, to get the truest picture of a child. Emotional factors, sometimes called non-cognitive factors, such as self-confidence or stress, must also be taken together with a child's neurodevelopmental profile. I once had a student who seemed to struggle with recalling information, making it appear as if he had challenges with short-term memory. I discovered only after speaking with his mother that he had anxiety about being wrong in front of his peers. When he needed to recall something, he would often just say that he could not remember. Anxiety can be hard to identify because sometimes there are no observable behaviors, as was the case with this child.

With this new information, I was able to try different ways of reaching him, which revealed that confidence, or lack thereof, did in fact affect his ability and willingness to recall. His challenge with recall was based more on emotional factors than a lack of encoding or consolidating of memory. Differentiating for him entailed encouraging him to recall only when the chances were high for him to have success. Allowing him to take increasingly larger chances as his confidence was gradually built up, while protecting him from negative peer responses should he make a mistake, was a way to differentiate for the part of him that was too afraid of showing his peers that he could be wrong.

Aside from demonstrating the importance of using a child's emotional state and readiness to interpret a neurodevelopmental profile, this example also helps illustrate the importance of communicating with parents for effective differentiation for young children.

St. Andrew's teachers are committed to Responsive Classroom practices, which value working in partnership with parents to help the child most effectively because we understand that both teachers and parents hold vital pieces of information about a child. Sometimes, when we consult with parents and share what we see at school, parents will share that they see similar types of behaviors at home. Other times, they may tell us that that they are able to do tasks with ease that we see them struggle with at school. Either way, the information parents bring to the table is essential in helping teachers refine our thinking about the child's learning profile, which in turn helps us differentiate in class.

As we form an understanding of individual students in the first weeks of school, we also see the learning profile of the class emerge. We differentiate according to not only the needs of individual students, but also the personality of the class, and we recognize that brain plasticity is a key mindset for both the teacher and the students. Strong lesson plans are created not in a vacuum but with real students in mind. Social studies lessons are particularly well-suited for modifying curricular content that appeals to students' interests, thereby increasing engagement. We also teach using multiple modalities, which makes learning fun, while allowing a wide range of learners to receive information in ways that sometimes challenge their current learning strengths and at other times challenge their current learning weaknesses.

Differentiation is not a supplement to the curriculum but a mindset that infuses all that we do to help our children meet their potential. This way of thinking entails that we work to establish, from the onset, an inclusive, culturally responsive classroom environment, where students can feel safe and take risks, knowing that the differences that make them who they are will be respected by their peers.

Finally, differentiation in the classroom does not take a break. As brains change and as individual and group needs change over time, so should how we differentiate. To do this, teachers must be attentive, open-minded and purposeful in continuously collecting new data and recalculating our approach to help a child succeed. Listen. Observe. Ask students to self-reflect. Children are incredibly resourceful beings, and sometimes they will find their own way of differentiation, if you empower them.

Sung Hee Kim teaches first grade at St. Andrew's.

Student Manifestos

As always, I look forward to fresh faces each September—particularly as the transition to third grade is always a special one at St. Andrew's. In the past, the second graders transitioned from one campus that housed the youngest students at St. Andrew's, and moved to the "big campus" in the fall. Now that we have expanded to become a one-campus school, third grade marks a transition from the first floor of our lovely new lower school building, shared by our preschool through second-grade students, to the second floor, which is the domain of the third through fifth graders. Looking at these apprehensive, curious, and innocent faces, I always wonder what their hopes and dreams for the new school year are, and what personality traits they will bring to the classroom that will make it a unique group of children.

St. Andrew's is a school that focuses on mind, brain, and education science, so it is expected that faculty use current research to inform their teaching practice. It has a side benefit of making St. Andrew's a really fun place to work. In third grade, we focus on growth mindset and student accountability as starting places as the students learn to define who they are as students, and what their personal responsibility is in their own learning.

Meanwhile, when the students enter the classroom, their parents do, too. I know, from years of experience, that the students have parents that practice parenting in equally unique ways, and this is a wonderful thing. I also know that each parent has their own hopes and dreams for their child's learning. Ahh, the joyous dilemma of third grade—that transition from one floor to another is also a transition in independence and metacognition, and it is work for both the students and the parents. How to get these students to take control over the part of their learning that they are developmentally ready for, and to start to define their life as a student in a way that is meaningful to them? How to help parents support their child in this time where increasing self-knowledge and independence as a learner is developmentally appropriate?

On alternate Wednesday mornings we delve a bit deeper into growth mindset, based on work by Carol Dweck,[67] and including materials created by Christina Winter.[68] In this program, students learn all about their brains and why they are unique as children and as learners. Using videos and read-alouds, we do multiple lessons on mindset that challenge the students to think deeper about their own learning.

Students think about the distinction between growth and fixed mindset by learning about different parts of the brain and what they do, that their brains change over time, how to grow their brains, and why students need to be vulnerable to have a growth mindset. Students learn how "hard things" help them grow and develop perseverance; how frequent check-ins with teachers are useful and effective for reflecting on their work; and that knowing that concepts like "grit" and "stamina" and "passion" are necessary to help them define who they are and what they stand for; and how the best way to grow a brain is through mistakes, and the power of "yet." The students love this work and I hear them using the positive terms when talking about their work and the work of others... while in the classroom.

Outside of class, this positive self-talk often disappears. In the hallway I hear students say to each other, "Ugggg, it's math time. I am really bad at math." Or, "I wish I could do like [insert student name] does. I stink at it." This agrees with Dweck's work, which says that growth mindset tends to be context dependent—I might have a growth mindset in this subject or at this time, but a fixed mindset in others. But Dweck also suggests that we can shift our mindset. So, I wondered, what could I do to help the students consistently apply the growth mindset lessons to their everyday

---

67 Dweck, C. S. (2006). *Mindset: The New Psychology of Success*. Random House.
68 Mrs. Winter's Bliss. (no date). "Category: Growth Mindset", https://mrswintersbliss. com/product-category/growth-mindset-7/.

experience, not just on demand in the classroom? That's where student manifestos came to mind.

After lessons on growth mindset, students create a visual representation of their thinking around growth mindset. After showing multiple examples, the students set to work on their iPads reflecting on their growth as a student. They use a soothing background, usually a picture, and then create "I am..." statements to place on their chosen background. They also search for meaningful quotes from some of their everyday heroes. Some write poems, often acrostic, to further define themselves. It takes weeks of reflection, going back and adding to or tweaking their manifesto before they create a final product for display.

As they do this work, students start to outline their unique strengths and accomplishments. They get in the habit of finding insights about themselves as learners as they go about their regular school day and use this to update their manifesto. The results are as varied as they themselves are.

Once done, we post the manifestos in the hallway, in the classroom, and on the front of their binders. They share their work with their parents and each other. They are proud, and should be, of their reflections. This project that started off about growth mindset has expanded into one that is also about metacognition, knowing about myself as a learner— and research suggests that metacognition is a very powerful research-informed strategy.

What's next? Digging deeper, of course! This year we will use some work of James Clear to further explore the meaning of habits and how to make the good ones stick.[69] Can we add this to our investigation of "Who am I as a learner? What strategies work for me?" Who knows what the students will create.

As one of my colleagues once stated, "Teachers are lucky, we are the only profession that gets to reflect and re-create each summer and welcome a new class each fall." Always a new class of fresh faces and new opportunities.

---

69   Clear, J. (2018). *Atomic Habits: An Easy & Proven Way to Build Good Habits & Break Bad Ones*. Avery.

Dale Kynoch teaches third grade at St. Andrew's.

The Relationship Between Reggio Emilia and Mind, Brain, and Education in a Pre-K and Kindergarten Classroom

For the past three years we have worked collaboratively in both formal and informal ways to explore the science of learning—mind, brain and education (MBE) science—for our youngest learners. Through our many conversations, recurring themes have emerged as anchors between research and practice. One of these anchors is the Reggio Emilia philosophy, and its practical wisdom approach to teaching and learning. In our most recent dive, looking into the research around classroom environment and student agency, we couldn't help but be reminded of some of the foundational principles of the Reggio Emilia philosophy. The relationship between MBE and Reggio is interesting and worth exploring more. The social nature of learning, the power of documentation for learning, children as active protagonists in their growing processes, and the importance of the environment and spaces where children are centered in learning[70] are some of the principles from Reggio Emilia that stood out to us.

The Reggio Emilia approach goes as far as to say that the environment is the "third teacher," alongside the educator and child.[71] The idea is that

---

70 https://www.reggiochildren.it/en/reggio-emilia-approach/.
71 Strong-Wilson, T. and Ellis, J. (2007). "Children and Place: Reggio Emilia's Environment as Third Teacher." *Theory into Practice*, 46(1), 40–7.

all incoming stimuli children perceive from the spaces they occupy, in classrooms or outdoors, impacts their learning, behavior, and well-being. In this approach, teachers orchestrate learning provocations, use documentation to make learning visible, and bring nature indoors for creative interactions in the learning environment.[72] Teacher-staged provocations encourage thinking and learning by inviting children to interact with objects and ideas that spark interest and prime the brain[73] for concepts to be further explored. Materials are selected and arranged in ways to provoke children to engage with them. In early childhood settings, this is a big part of the planning and preparation so important for high-quality teaching. All this aligns well with MBE principles, such as the science of motivation, which tells us that capturing a child's curiosity prolongs attention and increases engagement, both of which correlate with better learning outcomes.[74].

But this link to motivation is perhaps best illustrated with a story. In our pre-K classroom this fall we brought nature indoors to set up a seasonal provocation. Children were surprised to find an enormous pumpkin in our science center. The circular cut near the top invited them to pull on the stem and uncover its slimy pulp. They peered and smelled inside the pumpkin. "Can we touch in here? What are we doing with this?" children asked. Later that day, we carried the pumpkin to another table with assorted spoons, scoopers, and a blue towel. We listened, watched, and waited as the children began to touch and pull on the slippery insides. "Huh. Well, we can't get in there too well," one child said. After a brief conversation, the class decided to rearrange the chairs, so they could stand and reach in. As teachers, we made the choice to let the children explore their theories on how to access the pumpkin rather than giving them direct instructions at that moment. Some of the children were still having difficulty reaching the pumpkin, so several of them rolled the pumpkin on its side for a lower point of access. These young learners persevered in their thinking to find a workable solution that would allow

72 https://www.reggiochildren.it/en/reggio-emilia-approach/
73 Wexler, B., et al. (2016). "Cognitive Priming and Cognitive Training: Immediate and Far Transfer to Academic Skills in Children." *Scientific Reports*, 6, 32859.
74 National Scientific Council on the Developing Child. (2018). Understanding Motivation: Building the Brain Architecture That Supports Learning, Health, and Community Participation: Working Paper No. 14, www.developingchild.harvard.edu.

their investigation to continue! The pumpkin was a surprising addition to the classroom that generated excitement, stimulated problem solving, and prolonged attention on a single investigation.

To expand the learning potential of this classroom event, we used the Reggio-inspired approach to documentation, which makes learning visible by featuring the process of learning alongside the outcomes. It isn't just a record of what happened, but an interpretation of the learning that took place.[75] During our pumpkin investigation, we collected the traces of students' interactions with the pumpkin through photographs, and transcribed their dialogue throughout. We shared a slideshow that led to a lively discussion and made a wall display to document their learning. Our English language learners were very engaged, pointing out details in the pictures and using their new vocabulary, such as "stringy" and "goop." This documentation helped our class reflect on their involvement with the investigation, uncover new information in the images, and extend their thinking, all in a deeply social context. The children laughed about their interactions with the pumpkin, while the pictures of seeds fueled their desire to season and cook these pumpkin remnants in a large toaster oven. They later chose to take these cooked seeds home to share with their families, extending the joy from school to home. What's next? We have heard chatter about planting our saved seeds!

We know that making learning meaningful to the children's lives drives their agency and intrinsic motivation.[76] Furthermore, providing a platform for children to have a voice in their learning increases engagement and motivation, and through the Reggio Emilia lens, makes them the protagonists of their learning. This does not mean that it is free reign for the students, but rather, curriculum and experiences are built with their interests in mind.[77] It is a great example of the Reggio Emilia approach and mind, brain, and education science principles in alignment.

75 Project Zero, Harvard Graduate School of Education. (2006). Documentation and Display: What's the Difference? http://pz.harvard.edu/resources/documentation-and-display-whats-the-difference.
76 Kuhl, P. (2018). Learning and the Social Brain, 25 July, Edutopia. https://www.edutopia.org/package/learning-and-social-brain.
77 Barron, B. and Darling-Hammond, L. (2008). *Teaching for Meaningful Learning: A Review of Research on Inquiry-Based and Cooperative Learning*. Jossey-Bass.

A simple example of making learning meaningful and allowing students' voices happened this past October when our kindergarteners were learning the new phonics concept g says /g/. To make a connection to the /g/-sound, a homemade ghost crafted with tissue paper was brought into the classroom as an object that begins with the /g/-sound. As children passed the ghost around for each to look at and engage with (and say ghost begins with /g/), one of them stated that they wanted to learn how to make ghosts, so that we could decorate our classroom for Halloween. Instead of immediately saying, "Okay, let's make ghosts," the children were told that it was a great idea and we needed to think about when and how we could incorporate this idea into the week. As the teachers, we wanted to connect their idea of decorating the classroom with our curricular plan for the week. Making predictions and asking questions were two reading habit skills we planned to explore in the week ahead, and we chose to read a book about a haunted house that both helped us explore these reading habit skills and also generate ideas about how we could make our classroom look spooky. After the read aloud, the class had an opportunity to brainstorm their ideas, collaborate, create ghosts, and finally fill the classroom with these handmade decorations for Halloween.

Throughout these lessons, the simple act of sharing our creativity with the children inspired or motivated them to express themselves in creative ways as well.[78] This joyful learning is reflected in the Hundred Languages principle of the Reggio Emilia approach—the importance of providing children with many ways to share their thinking of the world around them. By providing the children with a platform to express their understanding of Halloween and how one can represent the symbols of it we gave them a voice to showcase and anchor their own learning.[79] Supporting our learners' agency connected to our phonics lesson enabled them to truly learn the concept g says /g/, as evidenced by their use of

78 Romero, C. (2015). What We Know about Purpose & Relevance from Scientific Research, July, *Student Experience Research Network* (formerly *Mindset Scholars Network*), https://nsiexchange.org/wp-content/uploads/2019/06/What-We-Know-About-Purpose-and-Relevance-.pdf.

79 Ryan, R. M. and Deci, E. L. (2000). "Self-Determination Theory and the Facilitation of Intrinsic Motivation, Social Development, and Well-being." *American Psychologist*, 55(1), 68–78.

this new knowledge in their reading and writing following the lessons that week. Giving the children a voice and pausing to figure out how to incorporate their ideas into our week's lessons, enabled us to have a deeper intent around what could be seen at a casual glance as simply a fun arts and crafts project.

For us, taking a deep dive into the science of learning has given us the confidence to boldly use the pedagogy synonymous with Reggio Emila in ways that we know will make learning stick for our youngest learners. Who would have thought that following the science of learning would have led to so much joy!

Vas Pournaras teaches kindergarten at St. Andrew's and Denise Kotek taught preschool at St. Andrew's during the writing of this article.

Part III

Secondary Part 1: Building the Foundations for Learning

To Planner or Not to Planner

On a very basic level, executive functioning is a set of mental skills that helps individuals complete tasks and effectively manage their time. Many articles refer to executive functioning as the CEO of the brain. The more we at St. Andrew's learned about mind, brain, and education science, the more we wondered, are there links among handwriting, memory, executive functioning, and helping students make sure all their assignments are completed and turned in?

Executive functioning is a set of skills that can be learned through careful, systematic instruction. Like muscles, these skills need to be flexed or practiced in order to be strengthened. For students, one of the greatest demands on their executive functioning, and thus the higher order thinking part of the brain associated with it, the prefrontal cortex, is how they plan each day to meet the various demands on their time: school, clubs, sports, music lessons, social life, and, importantly, sleep. Planners help students learn how to identify priorities, outline their short and long-term goals, and space out larger assignments into more manageable chunks.[80] Most of us, who were probably born before 1990, used to plan a day, week, month, or year using traditional paper planners. However, technology, including online calendars and virtual planners, now offers choice in how we "write down" what we must do. The question, then, for each individual student is, "Which planner type, paper or digital, is best for me as a learner?"

80 Brown, P. C., Roediger III, H. L. and McDaniel, M. A. (2014). *Make It Stick: The Science of Successful Learning.* Belknap Press.

Research tells us that when you write something down, you are more likely to remember it.[81] Why is this? Researchers think it is because when we write something down, we are thinking harder to make more deliberate decisions about what is important. There appears to be something about slowing down and making a judicious decision about what to write that helps things stick better in long-term memory. Research also suggests that reading traditional paper text has benefits over electronic books.[82]

While many students have turned to electronic tools to plan their lives, the research behind writing things down remains compelling. It is our hypothesis that the act of physically writing something may be the best way for most students[83] both to remember their assignments and improve their executive functioning skills. With the increase in online learning management systems (at St. Andrew's we currently use Schoology), the practice of writing down assignments has decreased. Students are no longer writing down their assignments in paper planners but instead are relying on digital mechanisms where the teacher is responsible for writing down the assignment. By doing this for the students, students are no longer actively engaged in the homework planning process, which may have two effects. First, they may not be as successful or efficient at planning their homework. Second, they are losing opportunities to increase their executive functioning skills.

Listening and writing activate the brain so that memory is enhanced; therefore, when students takes pen to paper and write down their homework when it's announced in class or written on the board, they are far more likely to remember it. It is also possible that physically writing down what needs to be completed each night might be a stress reliever because it allows the students to see exactly what needs to be done and when. Writing things down also frees up working memory, which is both

---

81   Meyer, R. (2014). "To Remember a Lecture Better, Take Notes by Hand", 1 May, The Atlantic, http://www.theatlantic.com/technology/archive/2014/05/to-remember-a-lecture-better-take-notes-by-hand/361478/.

82   Willingham, D. (2018). Electronic Textbooks: What's the Rush?, 2 April, *Daniel Willingham—Science & Education*, http://www.danielwillingham.com/1/post/2012/04/no-title.html.

83   We say "most students" in recognition that for some students, for a variety of reasons, the reverse may be true—but all students need to work at finding the strategy that works best for them.

limited and in high demand, which helps enable long-term planning and higher order thinking.

Effective use of paper planners may improve executive functioning skills by allowing kids to keep track of their homework and long-term projects, manage their time, chunk long-term assignments into smaller more manageable segments, gather the needed materials for homework and projects, set short- and long-term goals and self-monitor progress, prioritize, and reflect on previous actions and strategies. Research suggests that students interact with paper books and electronic books differently,[84] and we believe that the executive functioning skills we just mentioned might be more effectively practiced when students are interacting with the information in paper form. In part this is because the paper book forces them to interact with and manipulate the information, whereas in a digital format they are likely to be just consuming it, probably in a non-linear fashion.

In 2015, in a partnership between the Educational Center at St. Andrew's and the CTTL, we sought to apply research in executive functioning to design a new student planner.

In the SAES planner:

- students can see the weekly overview along with tabs for each trimester. Time management, which can be a challenge for even the most successful student, is all about planning and controlling the amount of time spent on activities. By having a weekly view along with grading period tabs, students can keep track of their assignments, make a plan for executing those assignments, and keep track of their time. This helps students see the "big picture" and better control and plan their time.

- students are able to prioritize their assignments in relation to when classes meet and when long-term projects may be due by being provided with the type of day on the weekly overview (and with each daily schedule in the back of the planner).

---

84 Daniel, D. B. and Willingham, D. T. (2012). "Electronic Textbooks: Why the Rush?", *Science*, 335, 1569–71.

- students are also able to look at each month "at a glance" and have a preview of the next week. This helps develop long-term planning skills and helps students manage their time.

- students can physically check off the boxes "completed" and "turned in" for each subject that the school day demands. Feedback from students suggests that the active process of checking off completed work creates a greater sense of accomplishment. Feedback from teachers and students told us that "completing" and "turning in" are two very distinct episodes, and identifying them as such helps ensure that both happen.

- students can number the order in which assignments and other tasks will be completed. This helps their time planning and prioritization skills.

- students can use the "undone from previous week" box on the left side of the page and the "weekend" boxes on the right side to see and organize their week, which allows them to chunk out their assignments into more manageable portions.

- students are set up for success with a "materials needed" box for each class that helps them arrive to school, and each class, ready to learn.

Every middle school and ninth-grade student begins each new school year with the St. Andrew's planner. In the first three years of the planner's evolution, we have observed an increase in the number of students regularly using the St. Andrew's paper planner as their go-to means of organizing their work. Emily Todd '17 shared her experience with the St. Andrew's paper planner:

It was by far one of the most effective tools I used daily throughout my time in high school. The planner became more critical to use as classes got harder. I went from simply writing assignments in the boxes to color coding everything and writing due dates to projects weeks in advance. There is so much going on in high school among academics, athletics, and social life that it is essential to use the planner in order to keep track of everything in one place. The St. Andrew's planner is different because it adapts every year to incorporate academic schedule changes and to fit the needs of the student body.

The planner is being used just as much by students who have strong executive functioning skills as those who currently do not, which is interesting, and we see as a sign that we did well in including the features we did. As pointed out in "We All Need Executive Functions," every individual has executive functioning strengths and challenges. Executive functioning is a crucial set of skills from which we can all benefit and improve. Developing a St. Andrew's, home-grown resource that aligns with research on executive functioning and memory that helps students organize and prioritize their work ultimately empowers students to become more efficient, confident, and independent learners who are in more control of attaining their goals.

A good planner is good for everyone.

Samantha Speier was the Director of the Education Center and a middle school academic dean at St. Andrew's during the writing of this research-informed article.

Breaking the Frozen Sea

During my first year of teaching high school English, I had a conversation with a parent that stands out in my mind. This parent had arrived in the afternoon to pick up her son and decided to swing by my room for a quick chat. We discussed the class in general and her child's progress. And then, finally, came a familiar question:

"Mr. Seidman," she asked, "aren't any of the books you assign happy books?"

I wanted to please her, but the truth is that I don't assign many happy books any year. Not all the stories we read give us a comforting sense of the world, nor should they. Some of the very best literary works are those that offer no easy answers and increase our feelings of uncertainty and unease.

While such novels and plays rarely end on happy notes, those works have a value to them that cannot be overstated. *One Flew Over the Cuckoo's Nest, Their Eyes Were Watching God, A Clockwork Orange, Invisible Man, The Awakening, The Road, The Great Gatsby, The Glass Castle*: these works were not written to make us feel comfortable in our worlds. But that's exactly the point. Sometimes it's important to embrace the fact that the way is hard and steep, and things don't always turn out the way we want them to.

It is that struggle that leads my students to think and rethink the nature of truth after reading *1984* or to wrestle with their preconceptions about the narrative of Western progress after reading *Things Fall Apart*. An increased understanding of the neurological shifts and developments that result from reading such works has reinforced my decision to teach these stories. In addition, learning more about mind, brain, and education science has spurred me to change my pedagogical approach. I now more consciously link reading and writing to developing students' capacity to empathize and effectively persuade others.

Social cognition refers to how people process, store, and apply information about other people and social situations. A wide range of skills are included within this neurodevelopmental category. For instance, students need to learn the art of verbal pragmatics to engage in code switching and humor regulation. In addition, students must develop collaboration and self-marketing skills as well as the kind of political acumen that allows students to nurture positive relationships with others.

The bedrock of many of the skills that we associate with social cognition is what psychologists refer to as "theory of the mind," the ability to put yourself in someone else's shoes to understand their perspective. Despite years studying language and its development, there is much that remains mysterious to us regarding what occurs in the brain when we read and write. However, recent studies indicate that the act of reading and writing is closely linked to the development of the "theory of the mind."

According to several research studies, it's not just the portions of our brain that process language that become activated while reading fiction. Rather, the prefrontal cortex that houses our moral development is particularly engaged, as is the left temporal cortex and other areas that orchestrate "embodied semantics," a process in which brain connectivity during a thought-about action mirrors the connectivity that occurs during the actual action.[85] For example, reading about swimming can trigger some of the same neural connections that fire when one is physically swimming.

More recent studies have revealed that those who read fiction score higher on empathy tests and tests for social acumen.[86, 87] Considering teaching reading and writing through this neurodevelopmental lens suddenly

---

85 Ryan, J. (2014). Study: Reading a Novel Changes Your Brain, *The Atlantic*, 9 January, https://www.theatlantic.com/education/archive/2014/01/study-reading-a-novel-changes-your-brain/282952/.

86 Flood, A. (2016). Literary Fiction Readers Understand Others' Emotions Better, Study Finds, 23 August, *The Guardian*, http://www.theguardian.com/books/2016/aug/23/literary-fiction-readers-understand-others-emotions-better-study-finds.

87 Kidd, D. C. and Castano, E. (2013). "Reading Literary Fiction Improves Theory of Mind." *Science*, 342(6156) (October 18): 377–80.

means that this teaching comes with an incredible new responsibility. When we teach students to read deeply, we're teaching them to open their hearts to other people's worlds, and when we teach them to write well, we are giving them the tools to foster empathy in others.

Viewing reading and writing as a way to cultivate my students' social cognitive skills opened up new possibilities to me as an educator. I now strive to assign work designed to nurture students' sense of empathy and understanding. After reading Shylock's famous "I Am A Jew" speech from *The Merchant of Venice*, my sophomore students are asked to compose their own "I Am" speeches, written from the perspective of someone else. Previous examples have included "I Am A Child Soldier," "I Am A Single Mother," and even "I Am An English Teacher."

As a capstone assignment after reading Arundhati Roy's *The God Of Small Things*, students compose a monologue from the perspective of one of the main characters, making the case that they are not to blame for the tragic events of the novel. After completing Truman Capote's *In Cold Blood*, seniors in my AP English Language class deliver speeches in which they are forced to defend Perry Smith in a court of law, asking the jury to empathize with the character and grant him mercy.

While I certainly continue to assign traditional essays in my class, these other sorts of assignments allow students to engage in a different kind of creative work, one that builds both their sense of empathy and their mastery of persuasive rhetoric.

Mind, brain, and education (MBE) science often validates existing pedagogical practices. In this case, however, MBE science also supports what fiction writers have observed about their own craft: the particular power of words to build our sense of empathy. It was the writer Franz Kafka who noted that "a book must be the axe for the frozen sea within us." In asking our students to read different and difficult voices and to write from new perspectives, we are teaching them to raise that very axe and break the frozen sea within themselves.

Andrew Seidman teaches upper school English at St. Andrew's where he guides the publication of the school's literary magazine, *Creaturae*. Andrew was a CTTL/Omidyar Teacher Research Fellow between 2016 and 2018 and is a Neuroteach Global Mission grader.

Emotion and Cognition

Every teacher knows how critical the opening days of school are, and in preparation for them, we run around setting up bulletin boards, building websites, composing lesson plans, mapping curricula, writing course expectations, and more often than not, waiting in long lines at the photocopier. It is the time of year when we think carefully about what we want to teach and how we want to teach it, and then take the steps to bring our vision to fruition. I believe that there are two other integral questions, however, that teachers often overlook but need to ask themselves as they head into the school year: how do I want my classroom to feel and what steps can I take to create this feeling in my learning space?

Students need to feel safe, seen, and valued in order for deep learning to take place. As Carissa Romero has argued, "students who are confident they belong and are valued by their teachers and peers are able to engage more fully in learning. They have fewer behavior problems, are more open to critical feedback, take greater advantage of learning opportunities, build important relationships, and generally have more positive attitudes about their classwork and teachers. In turn, they are more likely to persevere in the face of difficulty and do better in school."[88]

It is our task then as teachers to take deliberate and thoughtful actions to build trust and a sense of community in our learning spaces. What transpires in our classrooms during the opening weeks of instruction—how we speak to our students, the opportunities we offer (or don't offer) to them—conveys an unspoken and essential narrative. This is when our students develop their understanding of what happens in this space and

---

88   Romero, C. (2015). "What We Know about Belonging from Scientific Research." Mindset Scholars Network.

determine how they want to behave within it. As Lisa Quay has eloquently summarized, "almost every situation is open to interpretation, and how people make sense of things determines their behavior."[89]

Building a culture of trust and respect in the classroom begins with empathy, attention, understanding, and most importantly, a willingness to be flexible. Below are three tenets of this process; the list is by no means exhaustive, but will hopefully provide a helpful starting point for conscious and deliberate community building.

FOCUS ON THE GOOD AND CREATE SPACES TO SHINE

As the CTTL has noted, "teachers should work to not only increase positive emotions in the classroom, but to also limit negative emotions"[90] by using positive, inclusive, and encouraging language. This does not mean that we should stop being critical. Identifying areas for growth, communicating these clearly, and determining strategies that enable students to tackle challenges head-on are all essential practices if we want our students to learn and progress.

How we present this feedback to them, however, has a monumental impact on its efficacy,[91] and therefore teachers should strive to convey feedback in a way that "forestalls negative interpretations."[92]

By acknowledging and celebrating our students' achievements, we show them they are seen and valued, which in turn fosters positive emotions and builds self-efficacy. We can do this through our verbal communications, written feedback, or providing a space in the classroom for students to showcase their own successes, such as an "I'm Proud Of..." bulletin board. The latter is a particularly powerful tool, since it promotes

---

89 Quay, L. (2018). "The Science of 'Wise Interventions': Applying a Social Psychological Perspective to Address Problems and Help People Flourish." Mindset Scholars Network.

90 The Center for Transformative Teaching and Learning. *Classroom Culture: Field Guide*. Neuroteach Global.

91 Romero, C. (2015). "What We Know About Belonging from Scientific Research." Mindset Scholars Network, 4.

92 Quay, L. (2018). "The Science of 'Wise Interventions': Applying a Social Psychological Perspective to Address Problems and Help People Flourish." Mindset Scholars Network, 3.

a broader, self-determined definition of triumph and offers a space for public recognition.

READ THE ROOM AND BE FLEXIBLE

One of the simplest and most effective things we can do to foster empathy in the classroom is to provide our students with opportunities to communicate their feelings. Whether we ask them to circle their current emotional state on a Blob Tree, place a sticky note onto a Feelings Chart to communicate their mood (e.g., I'm great, I'm okay, I'm struggling), or do individual check-ins, we are conveying the crucial message that they are seen and cared for. It is also important to recognize that when students are in a heightened negative emotional state, it is hard for learning to happen.[93] As Mary Helen Immordino-Yang and Antonio Damasio have made clear, "any competent teacher recognizes that emotion and feelings affect students' performance and learning as does the state of the body, such as how well students have slept and eaten or whether they are feeling sick or well."[94]

Taking five to ten minutes to acknowledge this and provide students with outlets to release anxiety or shift their headspace, rather than ploughing ahead with a lesson, not only validates them, but also results in more productive learning afterward. By having a handful of stress-relief activities at the ready that are still connected to your content-area (in my case, this includes going outside to write out verb forms in sidewalk chalk or toss a beach ball to practice noun cases), you can help students refocus their energy and bring joy to the learning process.

STEP BACK AND LET THEM LEAD

Giving students a voice in the classroom, whether it is designing a project, leading a review session, or rearranging the furniture, helps build a sense of inclusion and investment in their learning space. When we invite students to be active participants in our classrooms, to share their thoughts on the

---

93 The Center for Transformative Teaching and Learning. (2019). *Classroom Culture: Field Guide*. Neuroteach Global.

94 Immordino-Yang, M. H. and Damasio, A. (2007). "We Feel, Therefore We Learn: The Relevance of Affective and Social Neuroscience to Education." *Mind, Brain, and Education*, 1(1), 3–10.

classroom culture and how this can be improved, we are communicating our belief in their abilities, showing our respect for their opinions, and creating a space where their needs can be vocalized and fulfilled.

By stepping back and allowing students to take the lead, we are also introduced to new vantage points—things we may have never seen or accounted for on our own. Asking students to create their own community norms or classroom expectations, for example, rather than dictating a list of rules to them, broadens the input, ensures more needs are being met, fosters a sense of inclusion, and promotes student interest in upholding these guidelines, since they were the authors of them.

Building a classroom environment of trust and respect, where students feel safe, seen, and valued, requires thoughtful and conscious planning, open communication, and the willingness to take risks and remain flexible. The effort invested in this process, however, has immediate and long-lasting results: a learning space where students can flourish and deep learning can take place.

Kristin Webster taught middle and upper school Latin at St. Andrew's during the writing of this research-informed article.

Belonging and Middle School

In her book *The Gift of Imperfection*, Brené Brown says "Belonging is the innate human desire to be part of something larger than us. Because this yearning is so primal, we often try to acquire it by fitting in and by seeking approval, which are not only hollow substitutes for belonging, but often barriers to it. Because true belonging only happens when we present our authentic, imperfect selves to the world, our sense of belonging can never be greater than our level of self-acceptance."[95]

As powerful as this definition of belonging is, it may, at first glance, seem almost impossible to implement in a middle school! Middle school has the worst reputation when it comes to belonging. Whenever I ask at a parent event who would like to go back to middle school, very few hands are raised. When I tell people I lead a middle school, they almost always offer their admiration and blessings for having to deal with what is one of the most difficult periods in child development. Middle school, typically, is where we often feel like the odd person out, where we often struggle to find ourselves and then to locate ourselves in the sea of selves emerging around us. One of the main developmental tasks of middle school is to find your people, the group to which your authentic self best belongs. And the journey to that can be paved with many stones.

As difficult as a belonging mindset can be to attain, especially at the middle school level, it is critical to academic achievement. Being seen, respected, and appreciated are key aspects of belonging. When students feel like they belong in their school and indeed even in a particular classroom, they

95   Brown, B. (2010). *The Gifts of Imperfection: Let Go of Who You Think You're Supposed to Be and Embrace Who You Are*. Hazelden Publishing.

work harder, engage more, develop more grit and ability to bounce back from challenges, and because of that, they achieve more.[96] Our brains are motivated to determine if we are in a space of belonging, and this investigation for clues of our own emotional safety in an environment can be a drain on cognitive resources, particularly when it has to be done every day, every time we switch classes. Uncertainty about belonging can produce anxiety that can manifest as lack of engagement, negative and aggressive behaviors, checked out and depressive behaviors, and ultimately, a mismatch between one's potential and one's achievement.[97] We all search for a sense of belonging, and our girls, students of color, and LGBTQ+ students often tend to be even more heightened around their need to feel a sense of belonging in our classrooms, cafeterias, and hallways.

So how does a middle school create a sense of belonging at a time when it feels the most elusive? At St. Andrew's, we begin our day with a sense of belonging by utilizing the Morning Meeting Greeting from Responsive Classroom, giving each student an opportunity to have someone say, "Good morning, Joey," and give a smile of welcome into the space. We do this informally when we see each other as well as in our divisional morning assemblies. And not only do we do it, but we teach the students why it is important and the value of having someone acknowledge your presence. We continue it at lunch, where each week we rotate the assigned seating chart so that everyone will have broken bread with everyone else by the end of the school year. And not only do we do it, but we explain to students that this reduces the amount of time and energy spent scanning the lunch room for a place where you belong, and it increases your chances of being kind to one another because the more you know and interact with each other, the less likely you are to make a flippant comment that could ruin someone else's day. And on a free seating day in our lunchroom, if you ask one of our middle schoolers what is the answer to the question, "Can I sit here?" they will say, in unison, "The answer is yes."

---

96   "Belonging." Mindset Scholars Network, https://mindsetscholarsnetwork.org/
learning-mindsets/belonging/.
97   "Mindset Kit—What Is Belonging?, Belonging for Educators." Mindset Kit, https://
www.mindsetkit.org/belonging/about-belonging/what-is-belonging.

We carry it into our sports program, where we support and reward teamwork over athletic prowess, honoring everyone's contributions. And, of course, we infuse it into our classrooms, where we practice constructive one-on-one feedback partnered with specific strategies for increased learning—signaling our individual knowledge of our students. We create a sense of belonging when we celebrate the student who went from a C- to a B- as much as we celebrate the student who maintained a solid A, because we recognize the hard work that both of them put in.

Students know they belong in a classroom when they:

- understand the classroom rules and norms.
- know how to do well academically and socially in the classroom setting.
- feel a sense of agency, control, predictability, and fairness over what happens to them in the classroom.
- know that, within reason, their needs—physically, intellectually, emotionally—will be seen and addressed in the classroom.
- feel permission to take risks, make mistakes, and still be allowed to be a full part of the classroom.
- feel like there is some connection between who they are and what the class is about, as well as between their selves outside of the classroom and their selves inside of the classroom.

We know students belong when, like our middle schoolers at St. Andrew's, they can't help but smile when they get to school in the morning, even as they complain about how early it is! In so many studies of achievement gaps and measures of academic success, the sense of belonging is a common positive factor.

Once people get over their shock at how much I truly enjoy running a middle school, they inevitably ask, "What do you love about working in a middle school?" The answer is always the same: the opportunity to make middle schoolers love the place they're in.

Dr. Rodney Glasgow was Head of the Middle School and Chief Diversity Officer at St. Andrew's during the writing of this research-informed article. Rodney is now Head of School at Sandy Spring Friends School and leads the NAIS Student Diversity Leadership Conference and is the founder of the National Diversity Practitioners Institute.

Is That a Threat?

Students took over the first day of August faculty meetings at St. Andrew's. Spearheaded by two rising seniors, a panel of eight students came to school (a week before they had to!) to share things teachers and coaches have said to them during their academic careers that made them feel safe and welcome or invalidated and threatened. My immediate takeaway was that students should be part of our professional development more often. My longer-term takeaway is a slow-burning awe at the power of language and an ever-increasing attention to how I use it. I teach science—not English—and I'm pointing that out because language is a double-edged sword we all wield.

Students can't learn or use what they've learned when they feel under threat—we know this intuitively, and fMRI studies confirm it. Chronic stress can damage the hippocampus, which has the all-important job of consolidating new information into long-term memory. On a more moment-to-moment basis, the amygdala, which is in charge of our fear response, acts like a cognitive train-track switch: when all is well it engages our prefrontal cortex, the home of working memory and engine of higher order cognitive functions. But when the amygdala perceives a threat, the switch flips to engage our more primitive hindbrain and send us into fight-or-flight survival mode.[98] Thanks to this switching mechanism, the kinds of thinking we most want our students to do (connection-making, planning, analysis, self-regulation, etc.) are only possible in the absence of threat.

---

98   Arnsten, A. F. T. (2009). "Stress Signalling Pathways That Impair Prefrontal Cortex Structure and Function." *Nature Reviews Neuroscience*, 10(6), 410–22.

What is a "threat" in a classroom context? For those of us fortunate enough to set physical safety concerns aside, I think of threat as the opposite of belonging: a signal from the environment that we interpret as "you don't belong here." Evolutionarily, belonging to a group was a life or death matter—and though times have changed, signs that we don't belong still send our amygdala into fight-or-flight mode.

To cultivate a belonging mindset at school, we need to be aware that it has multiple components. According to middle school students, a sense of social belonging and academic belonging are distinct from each other—and students may feel one, both, or neither.[99] It's easy to imagine how signals from a teacher can be a source of academic threat, and signals from classmates can be a source of social threat. I'm sure we've all witnessed students feeling academically threatened by each other. Teachers can also be a source of social threat when we fail to validate our students' identities.

Identity development—and identity threat—touch both the social and academic realms. Our students continuously grapple with their identities across all of the "big eight" social identifiers (including our students with normative/systemically privileged identities—there is a lot to come to terms with when you have a white racial identity, for example). This is a shared mandate of equity work and mind, brain, and education science: we need to build space for our students' identities in our classroom and be attuned to potential sources of identity threat so we can minimize them.

The language we use around identity, expectations, assessment, feedback, etc. is an easily accessible tool to buffer both social and academic threat. Beyond using inclusive language, in general (family rather than parents, folks rather than ladies and gentlemen, outside of school rather than home), there are unconscious beliefs students often hold that we may want to address head-on.

As multiple articles in this volume of *Think Differently and Deeply* touch on, emotion and cognition are inextricably interlinked, and a sense of

---

99   Green, M., Emery, A., Sanders, M. and Anderman, L. H. (2016). "Another Path to Belonging: A Case Study of Middle School Students' Perspectives." *The Educational and Developmental Psychologist*, 33(1), 85–96.

belonging is a critical ingredient for learning. I'm also suggesting that minimizing identity threat is essential to cultivate social and academic belonging in our schools. And rather than crossing our fingers and hoping students will feel our beliefs about intelligence and aptitude emanating from us—and hence understand why we push them with critical feedback, and why they should persevere through challenges without taking things personally—we can harness the power of language to state all of these things—explicitly, early, and often.

Eva Shultis teaches AP biology at St. Andrew's and is Associate Director of Program Development and Research for the CTTL.

COMMUNICATE HIGH STANDARDS WHEN GIVING CRITICAL FEEDBACK

Social psychologist David Yeager and his colleagues recruited 44 white and Black seventh-grade students who were earning Bs and Cs in social studies. They asked the students to write a personal essay and then gave them to their teachers to grade and write comments on. Before the teachers returned the essays, researchers randomly assigned the students to receive one of these two notes from the teacher clipped to the paper:

Control group
"I'm giving you these comments so that you'll have feedback on your paper."

Wise criticism group
"I'm giving you these comments because I have very high expectations and I know that you can reach them."

When offered the opportunity to revise and resubmit their essays, 72% of Black students and 87% of white students in the wise criticism group did so, compared to 17% and 62% of the Black and white control groups. Notably, wise criticism made the greatest difference for students who chronically self-reported lower levels of trust in the people, policies, and procedures of their school environment, and "seemed to slow the tendency for early mistrust to beget deeper mistrust for minority students."[100]

State your belief that all students have the potential to perform at the highest level in your discipline

In a series of studies across multiple university contexts, Aneeta Rattan and her colleagues found that women and historically underrepresented racial minorities in STEM courses reported a greater interest in and sense of belonging to that field if they perceived that their professors held the following beliefs:

- A growth mindset about intelligence (that intelligence is malleable and can increase with effort).
- A belief in universal aptitude for the discipline (that all people have the potential to succeed in STEM, in this case).

In two of Rattan's studies, students were presented with a fictional transcript of a professor welcoming them to the first day of a course, expressing a belief in either universal or non-universal aptitude for the subject:

Universal aptitude group

"I know that everyone has high intellectual potential in science, technology, engineering, and math. What this means is that the potential is there in all of you. I want each and every one of you to realize your potential."

Non-universal aptitude group

"I know that not everyone has high intellectual potential in science, technology, engineering, and math. What this means is that the potential is there in some of you. I want those of you who have this potential to realize it."

When the professor expressed non-universal aptitude beliefs, Black students reported lower interest in enrolling in the course than white

---

100 Yeager, D. S., Purdie-Vaughns, V., Garcia, J., Apfel, N., Brzustoski, P., Master, A., Hessert, W. T., Williams, M. E. and Cohen, G. L. (2014). "Breaking the Cycle of Mistrust: Wise Interventions to Provide Critical Feedback Across the Racial Divide." *Journal of Experimental Psychology: General*, 143(2), 804–24.

students, and women anticipated a lesser sense of belonging to the field than men. Both of these gaps were eliminated in the universal aptitude condition.[101]

DEPERSONALIZE STRUGGLE FROM IDENTITY

Gregory Walton and Geoffrey Cohen designed a series of interventions to bolster first-year college students' sense of belonging in their new schools. In one experiment, they presented a group of Black freshmen with the results of an upperclassmen survey, in which the responses of older students indicated two important points:

- That students of all racial identities had experienced academic hardship and doubt about whether they belonged in their first year.
- That these struggles lessened with time.

After being presented with evidence that the doubts and struggles they experienced were normal and not particular to them or their racial identity, this group of Black students reported a greater sense of belonging and belief in their potential to succeed (and went on to earn higher GPAs) than Black students in the control group.[102]

---

101 Rattan, A., Savani, K., Komarraju, M., Morrison, M. M., Boggs, C. and Ambady, N. (2018). "Meta-Lay Theories of Scientific Potential Drive Underrepresented Students' Sense Of Belonging To Science, Technology, Engineering, and Mathematics (STEM)." *Journal of Personality and Social Psychology*, 115(1), 54–75.
102 Walton, G. M. and Cohen, G. L. (2007). "A Question of Belonging: Race, Social Fit, and Achievement." *Journal of Personality and Social Psychology*, 92(1), 82–96.

Putting the Research on Student Emotions, Stress, and Achievement to Work in Classrooms and Schools

How can we help each individual student meet his or her peak potential? While there exist many answers to this question, as veteran educators and counselors, we know from research that there has been a precipitous rise in student anxiety in schools today, which increases the importance of schools to be as committed to what and how they teach as they are to the social and emotional needs of each of their students.

Students struggling with anxiety have become a major issue for school administrators, teachers, counselors, and parents. Writing in *The New York Times*, Alex Williams notes that according to the National Institute of Mental Health "some 38 percent of girls ages 13 through 17, and 26 percent of boys, have an anxiety disorder."[103] In schools all over the country, more students are struggling with anxiety disorders. For example, Susanna Schrobsdorff, writing in *Time* magazine, describes an uptick in anxiety disorders in high school students that has been noted since 2012: "It's a phenomenon that cuts across all demographics—suburban, urban and rural; those who are college bound and those who aren't."[104]

---

103 Williams, A. (2017). Prozac Nation Is Now the United States of Xanax, *The New York Times*, 10 June, https://www.nytimes.com/2017/06/10/style/anxiety-is-the-new-depression-xanax.html.
104 Schrobsdorff, S. (2016). "Teen Depression and Anxiety: Why the Kids Are Not Alright," *Time*, 27 October, http://time.com/magazine/us/4547305/november-7th-2016-vol-188-no-19-u-s/.

All people experience anxiety at times. It is an important self-protective mechanism that helps us determine unsafe situations. Related to the "fight or flight" response, anxiety is a warning signal indicating that there is danger in the environment. When a person struggles with an anxiety disorder, that fight or flight response is extreme and produces symptoms and behaviors that are more significant than the situation warrants.

School counselors commonly see several subsets of anxiety disorders—separation anxiety, generalized anxiety, performance anxiety, and social anxiety. When the problem is more serious, the anxiety can interfere with school attendance and performance.

Administrators and teachers along with school counselors have been thrust into the role of having to handle anxiety because of the increasing number of anxious students who come through our doors.

As Caine and Caine's book *The Brain, Education and the Competitive Edge* states, "Emotion is inseparable from learning... When we are under stress, it directs sensory intakes to our rear 'reactive brain' where our 'fight, flight, or freeze' response is embedded, and that automatic response from our evolutionary ancestors kicks in. This is sometimes called 'downshifting.'"[105]

Think about a school setting. How much learning sticks when a student experiences this downshifted state? Dr. Mariale Hardiman writes, "many students in our nation's schools are locked into this downshifted mode of thinking as a result of standard educational practices. Students are thus literally disconnected from their capacity for creativity and learning at high levels."[106] However, when we are under no or low stress, the limbic system that includes the amygdala directs sensory intakes to the prefrontal cortex, home of executive functioning and higher-order thinking.

How can schools best address this increase of anxiety among students? We must be proactive, we must educate, and we must make individualized plans at times.

---

105   Caine, G. and Caine, R. N. (2001). *The Brain, Education, and the Competitive Edge.* R&L Education.
106   Hardiman, M. (2012). *The Brain-Targeted Teaching Model for 21st-Century Schools* (1st edition). Corwin Press.

For the most part we know when and where the most anxiety-provoking times of the school year occur—beginning of the year, lunchtime, the end of grading periods, exams, and during oral presentations.

At St. Andrew's we have put some programs in place to address these anxiety-provoking times during the school year.

- Advisor Program—advisory groups of ten students meet two-to-three times a week. In this intimate setting, advisors get to know their advisees well. Periodic check-ins with parents can further help advisors to know which of their students struggle with anxiety.
- Advisors have one-on-one conversations with their advisees throughout the year. Advisors ask students to reflect on their strengths, challenges, and strategies for improvement. The personal connection through one-on-one conversations are crucial to student success and happiness.
- Some of our other advisory activities include: mindfulness training, physical activity—yoga, walking, basketball—as well as down time to reflect.
- Our bi-weekly Health Team Committee composed of the nurse, chaplain, school counselor, and the upper school administration helps us to identify and formulate strategies designed to help students struggling with anxiety.
- The school counselor meets yearly with the faculty to provide training on the signs of anxiety. Teachers are guided in designing their classes to be more inviting and less stressful.
- During the first two weeks of school, students are required to sit in advisor groups at lunchtime. This reduces social anxiety early in the year, especially for students new to St. Andrew's.
- Regarding public speaking: we encourage teachers to set up practice times with students with no grades, give them tips on classroom presentations, and equip them with strategies for speaking up in class.
- Classroom teachers are encouraged to meet with their students one-on-one periodically throughout the year. While meeting each individual student can take time from valuable class instruction,

the benefits for engagement, a feeling of belonging, and a more inviting classroom are far more productive in the long run for all students, anxious or not.

- For the more severe cases of anxiety, there needs to be an individualized support plan. Close communication with an outside therapist may be an essential part of supporting an anxious student within the school day. Students who experience panic attacks may need to establish a safe space within the school to regroup and get ready to return to class.

- Regular school attendance is the most important goal for anxious students. Avoidance creates more anticipatory anxiety.

Here are our top ten strategies for working with anxious students:

10. Use mindfulness and relaxation techniques to alleviate anxiety.

9. Utilize the advisor program, and the importance of strong positive relationships with adults in the school, to provide students an opportunity to discuss daily stresses.

8. Understand each student's current learning strengths and challenges, and how these can impact anxiety.

7. Empower students to manage their own anxiety and promote resilience.

6. When needed, create an individualized plan to manage anxiety during the school day.

5. Educate parents and faculty about anxiety.

4. Encourage students to attend school every day.

3. Remind students that avoidance creates more anxiety.

2. Help students confront their fears and accept them.

1. Strive to help students manage rather than eliminate anxiety.

As teachers, administrators, and school counselors, we know that a student's anxiety impacts his or her ability to learn. Schools that care for the social and emotional needs of their students are no less challenged; in fact, they are actually at the forefront of taking care of each student's well-being, which allows each student to enjoy even greater success in his or her academic pursuits.

Ginger Cobb is the Head of Upper School and Co-Director of Service Learning at St. Andrew's.

Jean Cohen was the school's counselor during the writing of this research-informed article.

Listening for Understanding: Building Trust–and Equity– in the Language

In her landmark book *Culturally Responsive Teaching and the Brain: Promoting Authentic Engagement and a Rigor Among Culturally and Linguistically Diverse Students*,[107] Zaretta Hammond underscores the crucial importance of trust as a prerequisite for learning.

"Trust and fear are inversely related," she explains. "Fear activates the amygdala and the release of cortisol [which] stops all learning for about 20 minutes and stays in the body for up to 3 hours."

Trust, on the other hand, "deactivates the amygdala and blocks the release of cortisol; [and] therefore frees up the brain for other activities such as creativity, learning, and higher order thinking."

All humans need to feel trust in order to learn and grow. Clearly, this is a key insight for teachers. And it is urgently needed. School is too often a place where students feel on edge and fearful; and those with marginalized identities all the more so.

But how do we build trust? And, in particular, how do we build trust in the language classroom?

---

107 Hammond, Z. L. (2014). *Culturally Responsive Teaching and the Brain: Promoting Authentic Engagement and a Rigor Among Culturally and Linguistically Diverse Students*. Corwin Press.

Language teachers have an incredible advantage because **we can use what we are teaching—the language itself—as a primary vehicle for building trust and relationships**. Indeed, that is what we should be doing if we are doing our job!

To develop proficiency, students need to be hearing and reading—or visually perceiving, in the case of ASL—input that they both *understand* and that they find *interesting*. They also need to have the opportunity to express themselves and be heard, both figuratively and literally.

Since communication flows much more easily in a positive relationship, it is only logical that the first area of focus in a language classroom must be to develop those relationships. How often have you found yourself at a loss for words and blanking on topics of conversation when you're talking with someone you're not comfortable with?

When we ask students to engage in a language that isn't their own—with the increased risk of looking foolish—the anxiety is all the greater. If we want students to develop proficiency in the language we are teaching, we need to give them opportunities to engage with the language **as a means of communication between people who care about each other**.

By developing trust, we create the conditions for all students to acquire language and be willing to take the risk of expressing themselves. Here are a few core practices that I have put into place in my classroom that have made a tremendous difference.

1. Listen for understanding: When students speak, listen to connect rather than to correct.

Trust begins with listening. By listening for meaning, we naturally respond in a way that is life-affirming and trust-forming. This is a significant change from how many of us were trained as language teachers and it is a powerful shift. By responding with real interest to what a student is saying, you'll be able to provide that student (and others in the class) with high-quality input that is comprehensible, interesting, and validating.

2. Curiosity and appreciation: Look for reasons to be surprised, delighted, and grateful.

Rather than looking for what's missing in what a student offers—a deficit approach—we can look for what's there. What amazing things did they do on the weekend? What was this student able to say today that they weren't able to say yesterday? Asking questions about how the students are and what's new with them today—*and really being interested in their answers*—provides rich soil for trust to grow and for language to develop.

3. Mutual trust: What do I need? What do you need? What do we need?

One of the things that is challenging for the flow of communication in any group is that different people have different sensitivities and needs. How can I know for sure what the people in the room need if I don't ask them? How will others know what I need for trust if I don't tell them?

Last summer I attended a week-long workshop with Cécile Lainé and experienced firsthand a powerful process for building mutual trust.[108]

Cécile wrote the word "trust" on the board in French (*la confiance*), and then held up a sign on which was written "Listen with your eyes, your ears and your heart." She explained, slowly and in French, that this is what she needed for trust. Then she asked us: what do *you* need for trust? We each wrote on a small piece of paper what we needed—in English or in French. After giving us the option of keeping our offering anonymous, she shared each of the needs with the class, expressing deep appreciation and gratitude. Speaking in French, she made sure everyone understood fully and that she was "getting" what was being expressed. When we were satisfied, she wrote the needs on the board. This became a poster that hung in the classroom. Over the course of the week, we celebrated when needs were met. Cécile also checked in with us to see how we were doing on trust at the end of each lesson that week—with our eyes closed, we held up fingers to show how much trust we were feeling, from 1 (uncomfortable/ low level of trust) to 5 (fully comfortable/high level of trust).

---

108 Laine, C. (2021). "Sharing Power with Our Students, Building Trust in the Classroom, Toward Proficiency," 23 August, https://towardproficiency. com/2021/08/23/sharing-power-with-our-students/.

159

When I brought this back to my own classroom in September, I was gifted with an important experience. In one class, a student had shared that they needed to know there would be no cold calling in order to feel trust. A week later, when I was asking students to talk about how they were doing, I felt discomfort radiating from one of the students and realized that since I wanted to hear from every student, this might be seen as cold calling! I stopped and walked over to the poster. I said, I think I might be going against one of our requirements for trust. I explained what my intention was—that I really wanted to know how they were doing and that there was no "wrong" answer. After some discussion, the student who had been showing signs of discomfort took a breath and agreed, but he made an important request: that I please not say "who's the next victim," because the word "victim" felt really intimidating. I'd said that for years, thought it was funny, and had no idea that it could be adding an additional layer of stress for some students. That student has become one of the most vocal students in the class!

Listening for understanding; showing curiosity and appreciation; and **creating authentic opportunities for mutual trust**: these are ways to meet core human needs.

When taken into the context of the classroom, it becomes clear how rarely these needs are given their full weight in education. If our pedagogy is to be truly equitable, we must recognize that everyone in the room is a full human with their own needs and sensitivities.

As language teachers, we have the privilege of our subject matter being language and communication. By truly listening for understanding and building trust, we can transform the language classroom from a place enjoyed by a talented few to a safe, inviting and enriching place where everyone knows they belong.

Dr. Anna Gilcher teaches Spanish at St. Andrew's.

Boosting Investment and Motivation

How often do you hear someone say "I took (insert language here) throughout high school and middle school, but I can't use it?" As a language educator, a little part of my soul is crushed every time I hear that. And yet, I can relate. My own language-learning journey was an arduous process.

Due to cultural norms in my family, I "learned" Hebrew for 10 years and French for three, but can't functionally use either. In ninth-grade, I chose Mandarin Chinese—a logical choice for someone who was having trouble with language, right? Fast forward 20 years later, and I'm a Mandarin Chinese teacher. So, what happened? When I chose to learn Mandarin, it was internally motivated. The reason for my investment went beyond external factors.

As a high school language teacher with my background in language learning, I am painfully aware of students feeling like they have no choice. After all, that was exactly how I felt in my French and Hebrew classes. Even though Mandarin was hard, I stuck with it. Research shows that providing carefully constrained choice in learning can increase student investment and motivation.[109, 110] But what are the limitations? How much can this actually boost motivation?

During the 2018–2019 school year, I set out on a journey to explore these questions about choice and investment in several levels of my Mandarin

---

109 Deci, E. L. and Ryan, R. M. (2000). "The 'What' and 'Why' of Goal Pursuits: Human Needs and the Self-Determination of Behavior." *Psychological Inquiry*, 11(4), 227–68.

110 Whitman, G. and Kelleher, I. (2016). *Neuroteach: Brain Science and the Future of Education*. Rowman & Littlefield.

classes. The Self-Determination Theory described by Deci and Ryan suggests that motivation is on a continuum, from amotivation on one end, to various forms of extrinsic motivation in the middle, to intrinsic motivation on the other end.[111] As a teacher, I wanted to figure out how to use choice to get my students to the far right of that continuum, which describes self-determined intrinsic motivation—motivation for enjoyment inherent in the task itself. I wondered if I could use proper scaffolding and socially-mediated processes to guide students toward intrinsic motivation.[112] Vygotsky clearly identifies the importance of social interaction in learning through the "zone of proximal development" (ZPD), and unless a learner has support from other artifacts or opportunities, known as affordances, they will not be able to learn.[113, 114] In other words, students will not be motivated in a class unless they feel the learning is "meaningful and worthwhile."[115] But what does this look like in a curriculum for required classes?

In my Mandarin II (high novice/low intermediate, typically sophomores) and Mandarin III (mid intermediate, typically juniors) classes, we cover roughly eight units throughout the year. Every other lesson, I allowed students to engage in what I called a "deep dive"—so that "deep dive" units were interspersed with "treatment as usual" units where I instructed students how I normally taught. In a "deep dive," students went deeper into a tangentially or directly related sub-topic of the unit. I helped them find an authentic resource as a starting point, and they had to use learner tools to find unknown vocabulary and grammar patterns. While I was there to help, I had to get very comfortable with not knowing all the answers, but being able to help find the answers. Students then were given an open-ended common question to show what they had learned.

111 Deci, E. L. and Ryan, R. M. (1985). *Intrinsic Motivation and Self-Determination in Human Behavior.* Plenum.

112 Little, D., Ridley J. and Ushioda E. (Ed.). (2003). *Learner Autonomy in the Foreign Language Classroom: Teacher, Learner, Curriculum and Assessment.* Authentik Language Learning Resources.

113 Vygotskij, L. S. (1986). *Thought and Language.* MIT Press.

114 van Lier, L. (2000). "From Input to Affordance: Social-interactive Learning from an Ecological Perspective." In J. Lantolf, *Sociocultural Theory and Second Language Learning,* Oxford University Press, 245-69.

115 Brophy, J. (2004). *Motivating Students to Learn.* Lawrence Erlbaum.

One example came during our unit on food. A student chose to tackle a recipe for cookies in Chinese. I helped her in several ways, which is where the scaffolding and ZPD were present: I showed her how to search the web for a recipe in Chinese, I reminded her how to identify words she did not know and how to use a language corpus to see those words used in other real world, authentic language examples, and I showed her how to identify and learn about common grammar patterns in the recipe. She had to create a unit of study based on that recipe, which required metacognition: what would someone need to know to learn this, what are the key words, and key concepts? As a test of her knowledge, she had to explain how to make these cookies in written form without any vocabulary aides, and then have a conversation with me about the recipe and cooking in general. In her self-reflection, she noted that she was able to feel engaged instead of just reviewing past words and she was relaxed and at ease because she could practice and learn more about baking.

I conducted an action research study to measure the impact of units where I used a "deep dive" approach, comparing these to my "treatment as usual" normal practice units. I adapted a published, validated survey to measure motivation, and also collected qualitative data from students. Students generally reported feeling engaged and empowered, as well as gaining ownership, after taking part in these projects. I also noticed an increase in performance on units in which we did not have "deep dives." It felt as though allowing choice in a controlled way allowed students to perform better even in units they were not as interested in. Analyzing the engagement data I collected showed a statistically significant increase in motivation in the "deep dive" units, with a pretty good effect size of 0.4. One potential flaw I noticed was that for this type of project, higher level and older students performed better. This could be due to age and maturity or level of language competency. As is often the case with research, the project you do generates more questions to be addressed by future work.

Evidence suggests that my "deep dive" approach did increase motivation, and led to an increase in performance. But it is quite a different type of teaching. Generally, this lack of control makes many teachers anxious. People say "but if student one does not know the same information as student two, how can you run the class?" The reality is that even in our first language, we do not know all the same content or have all of the same information as our interlocutors. We can perhaps imagine a core of knowledge that all students should know, but beyond that there are rings of more specialist, detailed knowledge; some students will know some of these rings, others will know others, and that's okay. I can talk to people in Chinese about my own interests such as gardening, but I've never driven a car in China and do not find great joy in cars, so I have a difficult time engaging in conversations about cars in both languages. Why should learning a second language be any different? Maybe it's time to get comfortable with being uncomfortable.

Sara Graham taught Mandarin Chinese at St. Andrew's during the writing of this research-informed article.

Advocating for Student Voice Is No Longer Enough: Now Is the Time for Students to Have Agency Over Their Learning

During a time where school districts, school administrators, teachers, parents, and families scrambled to figure out the best course of action to take—to ensure students were able to learn during an historic pandemic—one of the least considered factors that was taken into consideration was what *students* actually needed to continue their academic journey. Yes, some schools were able to pivot pretty seamlessly and offer, depending who you talk to, a learning experience that mimicked one that took place inside a school building. However, for those individuals who did not attend a school that was resourced with the infrastructure to attend classes virtually in a pseudo normal manner, there is validity in asserting that their learning became more of a word, than a reality. In fact, those highly resourced schools went even further to show what they perceived students needed during this time, by force feeding them into believing hybrid, synchronous, and/or asynchronous learning was the best thing for them at this particular junction in their learning process.

Whether you are smirking in some sort of laughter, shaking your head in disbelief, or finding the aforementioned in a state of uncertainty, and not sure what to think, just know that students' learning or lack thereof is and continues to be at stake.

For those of you who think that this article is about banishing school officials for creating learning opportunities for students during unprecedented times, the answer is, no! Or, for those who think that this is freedom to place blame on classroom teachers' efforts, and tireless commitment to learn new modules to the tune of Google Meet, Google Classrooms, Zoom links, Nearpod, and so forth, to bring a robust learning experience to their students, the answer is absolutely not! The purpose is to simply get us, as educators to absolve ourselves from believing that our professional titles, tenured status, and academic credentials takes precedence over our students' perspective and voice, and to start believing that our young learners need to be heard and listened to regarding what they perceive is applicable to their current, sustained, and future learning.

As an educator, with over 15 years of experience in this profession, where I've served students in public, charter, and private schools, along with time spent in college classrooms and teaching adult learners looking to earn their General Education Diploma (GED), I've always committed my pedagogical and andragogical practices toward advancing students' human, social, and cultural capital. My thought process was that by resourcing them with the knowledge and skills that were transferable in and out the classroom, they will not only be positioned to maximize their life's potential, but they will also develop a love for becoming a lifelong learner.

Accomplishing this feat, I was unapologetic about developing and advancing students' voices. This was true whether my students were adults or children. My premise was based on the findings in my dissertation investigation and publication out of the Harvard School of Education, in that when students' opinions are welcomed in the classroom, not only does the school thrive, but that institution's learners are also destined for lifelong success.[116] Moreover, by carving out intentional space for students to voice their ideas, concerns, interest, and the like "create[s] programs and policies that are more effective at meeting the school's own goals for supporting young people in their healthy development."[117]

---

116 Shafer, L. (2016). "Giving Students A Voice." Retrieved from https://www.gse.harvard. edu/news/uk/16/08/giving-students-voice. See also: Waters, K. D. (2015). A Mixed Method Case Study of Factors that Contribute to Black Male Students' Academic Achievement and Postsecondary Matriculation Rates. (Doctoral dissertation).

117 Ibid.

Although this is still my mantra, and because I believe as an educator, I, too, have to evolve; I can no longer assert that advancing student voice is sufficient enough to meet the diverse needs of our learners. I now posit that we as educators, administrators, and those responsible for drafting policies and curricula have to go a step further and begin advocating for *learner agency* to become common classroom practice. Please note that *learner agency* will be used interchangeably with *student agency*.

According to a publication in the Oxford University Press, "learner agency refers to the feeling of ownership and control that learners have over their own learning."[118] Further, when students are provided *agency* over what their schooling looks and sounds like, and how their curriculum is instituted, their level of engagement and confidence is enhanced, thus serving as a vehicle for learning that is more edifying.[119] Learner agency also aligns with the "autonomy" component of Deci and Ryan's self-determination theory of motivation.[120]

If one needed additional reasons as to why *learner agency* is essential to developing and advancing students' capacities, this phenomenon also adheres to assuring the curriculum is socially, civically, and culturally constructed.

At my current school, where each teacher receives training on mind, brain, and education (MBE) through our Center for Transformative Teaching and Learning (CTTL), we are currently engaged in a curriculum and pedagogy audit, or review, depending on who you talk to about this process. In the midst of this undertaking, the school is looking at ways to integrate MBE's research-informed instruction with our school's commitment to diversity, equity, and belonging (DEB); and how both ideologies can show up in our curriculum. With that in mind, ensuring *learner agency* is a focal point—the toiling of MBE and its connection to DEB can seamlessly coexist.

118 Oxford University Press. (no date). *Learner Agency: Maximizing Learner Potential.* https://elt.oup.com/feature/global/expert/learner-agency?cc=us&selLanguage=en.
119 Ibid.
120 Ryan, R. M. and Deci, E. L. (2000). "Self-Determination Theory and the Facilitation of Intrinsic Motivation, Social Development, and Well-being." *American Psychologist*, 55(1), 68–78.

The impetus associated with this belief is grounded in a number of MBE's power strategies, such as:

- Moving beyond lecturing
- Connecting class to students' lives
- Including choice
- Understanding the link between emotion and cognition
- Minimizing classroom threats
- Helping to grow executive functioning
- Combining joy and rigor
- Building students' metacognition skills
- Exploring beyond growth mindset

The identified power strategies are important to document, because when looking at how instruction is implemented through a DEB lens, *learner agency* can be that catalyst for having a curriculum that is student-centered, and one that meets the diverse needs of all students.

Before explaining the tenets of *student agency*, it is important to grasp what DEB or what culturally relevant instruction looks like in a curriculum and classroom.

Simply stated, providing students ownership of their education; creating safe space to allow students to bring their authentic selves to class, without fear of being prejudged by their peers or you as the teacher; purposely introducing diverse text throughout the academic year, that mirrors your student-body's racial, cultural, and lived experiences; recognizing and respecting students' learning styles, passions, and what interests them; and helping students understand the sociopolitical systems that is prevalent in and around their school are some of the essential elements to ensuring you are teaching through a DEB framework.[121]

When students are able to see themselves in a school's curriculum, this provides them with a sense of belonging that materializes in a number of affirmative ways that are both tangible and intangible. Murphy et al.

---

121 Fuglei, M. (2014). "Culturally Responsive Teaching: Empowering Students Through Respect." Resilient Educator, 11 June, https://resilienteducator.com/classroom-resources/culturally-responsive-teaching-empowering-students-through-respect/.

(2021) suggest: Students who feel a strong sense of belonging are more engaged and more likely to join school organizations, take on research opportunities, and make connections with peers, faculty, and staff.[122] Not only that, students who feel like they belong in school earn higher grades and opt into and succeed in more difficult courses. Murphy et al. (2021) also add that "belonging and connection in the classroom contribute to success and well-being, particularly for marginalized students."[123]

Considering the factors that were highlighted to contribute to student success and their overall socioemotional health, there is validity in recognizing that *learner agency* has a space in this discussion, especially when policy and curricular decisions are being made. To contribute to agency, learners need:

- scaffolding, support and information to make strong choices;
- options and opportunities to learn and to direct their own learning; and
- environmental conditions that allow them to exercise agency.

For instance, I pride myself on creating a classroom environment that is welcoming, challenging, and supportive. However, I'd be remiss if I did not note that many of my students who enter my classroom for the first time find a certain level of angst when they hear my instructional norms and style. Not to say that their anxiety is not warranted, because I can imagine how a student who has been trained to believe that rubrics, scripted curricula, and answering close-ended questions are the keys to their palpable success would feel, if they learn that I essentially do the total opposite.

Correct, I do not provide students with rubrics; I instead give them guidelines and objectives to reach. This not only develops their critical thinking skills but also affords them the opportunity to determine what they perceive is right or wrong. Do I help them grapple with the

---

122 Murphy, M. C., Boucher, K. and Logel, C. (2021). "How to Help Students Feel a Sense of Belonging During the Pandemic", 19 January, *Greater Good Magazine*, https://greatergood.berkeley.edu/article/item/how_to_help_students_feel_a_sense_of_belonging_during_the_pandemic.
123 Ibid.

assignments, yes, but do I give them concrete answers, no! I want students to take ownership of their learning, be uncomfortable knowing that there is not always one solution, and realize that at the end of this learning process, they will be prepared to meet the social, civic, and professional demands of life.

Moreover, *learner agency* equates to one being afforded the opportunity to engage in activities that are purposeful and relevant to a student's interest.[124] Simply stated, "student agency gives voice and often, choice, in how they learn" and as a result, giving them autonomy to make such decisions, "triggers a greater investment of [schooling], interest, and motivation."[125] Therefore, if educators, parents, and the like are truly committed to advancing students' outcomes beyond the classroom, *learner agency* should always be the center of their conversation. This is essential, because in the interim, this will help students learn more effectively and efficiently, and in the long term, agency will aid in helping learners become more confident, productive lifelong learners, and change agents outside of the classroom."[126]

Dr. Kenneth Waters taught English at St. Andrew's during the writing of this research-informed article. He was also the Upper School Diversity Coordinator and coached basketball.

124 Renaissance. (no date). *Student Agency*, https://www.renaissance.com/edwords/student-agency/.
125 Ibid.
126 Ibid. See also: Fuglei, M. (2014). "Culturally Responsive Teaching: Empowering Students Through Respect." Resilient Educator, 11 June, https://resilienteducator.com/classroom-resources/culturally-responsive-teaching-empowering-students-through-respect/.

We All Need Executive Functions

One thing became very clear when the Center for Transformative Teaching and Learning started facilitating workshops for teachers and parents: if you begin talking about the brain and its role in learning, large swathes of the audience jump to the conclusion, and stay mired in the erroneous assumption, that you are talking solely about students with significant learning challenges or special needs students. It is one of the most pervasive myths about mind, brain and education (MBE) science. So, a part of the mission of the CTTL is to bust this myth.

This is not just our opinion. There is a growing base of research showing that strategies for teaching and learning informed by MBE—actionable things that teachers and students should do and should not do—lead to better learning outcomes for all students. These strategies benefit not only those with learning challenges, but also the highest achieving (the Advanced Placement level student), as well as the "just fine" kids who are often overlooked when we think of ways to improve learning. Mind, brain, and education science-informed strategies work for all students.

There are two words you can add to a sentence containing "learning" and "brain" to make the audience even more convinced that you are only talking about students with learning challenges, and they are "executive functioning." In truth, who were you thinking of when you saw that this article was on executive functioning?

"Executive functioning" is a term that rarely seems to be used in a positive sense and is often followed by the word "disorder." It is also a term that is often used without being defined, as though there is some unspoken agreement that, to save everyone's collective embarrassment, no one in the room is allowed to ask, "what exactly does that mean?" When we understand more about executive functioning and the brain, we will see that it is an area of huge potential to improve learning outcomes for all students.

So, what is executive functioning? It is the ability to plan, organize, and execute. Take a moment to think of a project you are currently working on, and then think of all the steps you are taking to accomplish it. This is executive functioning: forming objectives, devising plans to meet these objectives, selecting the necessary cognitive skills, coordinating these skills, applying them in the correct order, monitoring and evaluating progress toward the objective's goals, making adjustments as necessary, and assessing when you have reached a satisfactory endpoint. These things are critical for every person to be a good student, but also, as we get older, to be an effective employee and a functioning member of society.

The frontal lobes of the brain play an important role in executive functioning. This region is one of the last in the brain to fully develop, still undergoing significant development until the mid-twenties at least, with rewiring of neural connections continuing throughout adult life. This means that all the way through schooling—through elementary school, through secondary school, through college, through a master's degree and into a PhD even—the prefrontal cortex is still significantly developing. While there is a large genetic component, this development, all the way through, will be affected by the environment, by experiences the student has, and by how they reflect upon and unpack those experiences. This is the concept of neuroplasticity, and it is something that schools, for better or for worse, whether they sign up for it or not, play a role in. The decisions that teachers make help shape, among other things, each student's executive functioning skills, regardless of whether an individual teacher believes this or not. We need teachers who both believe this and teach in ways that help students' executive functioning skills grow stronger. Schools and teachers are brain changers.

Let's look more closely at the executive functioning skills schools can influence the development of: problem solving, prioritizing, thinking ahead, self-evaluation, long-term planning, calibration of risk and reward, and regulation of emotion. These are skills that all students, the most advanced student, the "just fine student," and the struggling student, can benefit from being as good at as they possibly can be. But instead of embracing this opportunity to teach a raft of valuable school, job, and life skills, schools dare not talk about executive functioning for fear of, at best, the discussion being labeled as all about learning disabled students, or at worst, the school itself being labeled as an institution for learning disabled students.

Schools have a prime window of time during which they can influence the rewiring of students' brains. Unfortunately, schools either ignore or are ignorant of the research, and just leave this neuroplastic brain development to chance. Elementary schools do a better job teaching executive functioning—elementary teachers tend to recognize that these skills are a vital part of learning. What we need is for teachers to find age-appropriate ways to develop these skills at all grade levels.

What does the deliberate teaching of problem solving, prioritizing, thinking ahead, self-evaluation, long-term planning, calibration of risk and reward, and regulation of emotion look like in middle school and high school? What does it look like in history? In science? In math, language, or English? The articles "Google, Shoes and Inquiry" (available at www.thecttl.org) and "From Grant to Great Works" (pg 265 of this volume of *Think Differently and Deeply*) give good examples of how this is done at St. Andrew's. Think of somewhere in your own class where there is an opportunity to include some deliberate scaffolding to aid the development of these skills. Context is vital—it needs to fit authentically into your class and be linked to a topic of study—don't just announce, "this week we are working on an executive functioning project…" The scaffolding, of course, can be removed over time, and on an individual basis—too much scaffolding creates boredom, too little creates frustration. Each student has different needs, and these needs vary over time.

The good news is that the kind of assignments we need to purposefully develop these skills, and the way we need to structure and scaffold them, are, when we look at a broader range of MBE research, great teaching strategies. They are the kind of things we should be doing anyway, regardless of the executive functioning benefit. For example, teaching and assessing in multiple modalities, varying the neurodevelopmental demands we are placing on students over time guided by the content we are trying to teach, using arts integration to aid knowledge transfer and memory consolidation, teaching memorization strategies alongside material that needs to be memorized, giving prompt and scaffolded feedback, the opportunity to redo work, and providing chances for reflection. And, as we provide students with opportunities to plan, organize, and execute, the processing skills that lead students to their final goal need to be put on a higher pedestal—taught more explicitly and rewarded more.

Remember, if teachers choose not to do this, their students' prefrontal cortexes, every one of them, will be developing away in reaction to their environment and experiences. Their executive functioning skills will be necessarily changing, but we will be leaving the building of these critical student and life skills more to chance than we need to. So, the real nugget of gold that is "executive functioning for all" is that we can help all young people, at all ages of schooling—the most advanced student, the "just fine student," and the struggling student—to rewire their brains to become better learners and higher achieving students. Or we can make the deliberate choice not to.

Executive functioning isn't a disorder; it is something for all.

Dr. Ian Kelleher teaches science at St. Andrew's, is the Dreyfuss Family Chair of Research for the Center of Transformative Teaching and Learning, and is co-author of the book *Neuroteach: Brain Science and the Future of Education*.

Part IV

Secondary Part 2: Getting It In: Building Knowledge That Is Durable, Usable, and Flexible

How I Teach AP US History (Now)

I remember the panic I felt early in my first year of teaching Advanced Placement US History in 2002 when I walked into my classroom one Monday morning to find the notes that I had arduously written on every available piece of chalkboard had been erased. Copying the notes took me an hour and a half on Friday afternoon, and I felt good that both of my Monday block period classes (80 minutes) were prepped. The lesson plan was simple; I would read the notes as students copied them, adding some pithy anecdotes along the way to pique their interest. After all, this is largely how I had learned history in both high school and college. But with notes gone, what was I going to do? Who was responsible for sabotaging my students' learning in such an egregious way?

I have come to realize that the saboteur was me.

While the perpetrator was never found, I think back to that time with a good degree of embarrassment and guilt. The information dump pedagogy (sometimes code named "drill and kill" by teachers) that I employed early on in my AP teaching career was more about me than my students. I lectured to cover content. It wasn't as much about what the students learned as much as me being able to say "I covered that." For the students with excellent focus, attention, and memory, it worked. But for many, if not most of my students, these extended lectures resulted in glazed looks, boredom, and little recall of historical content, and ran counter to the research on how students learn best.

In the last 12 years, thanks to maturity, professional development, and training in mind, brain, and education science, my philosophy and teaching has evolved. First, I lecture far less, and when I do, I follow the concentration rule, never lasting more than 20 minutes. Lecturing still has its place in the classroom but must be used cautiously. If my job is in part to prepare students for a college history class, many of which are still lecture based, then I need to prepare my students for this methodology. When I do lecture, I give students a skeleton of the content on the smartboard and make the notes available for them afterward.

But I have largely moved away from notes and lectures in my class, opting instead for more active learning. Class discussions have supplanted lecture, and our reading of Howard Zinn or Paul Johnson never ceases to engender spirited debate. I try as best I can to provoke students by discussing perspectives they have not heard and at times may not want to hear. I have found attaching emotion, including antagonism, to a discussion improves memory retention and engagement. I am lucky, however, that I average about 15 students per AP class. This allows everyone to participate on a regular basis. For those students who are more reluctant, I will mix in a Fishbowl discussion or use "poker chips" (which they must spend before the end of class by participating in the discussion) to draw more reticent participants into the mix.

I have also used more group work. I will give groups (two to five students) a primary document to analyze, an historian's perspective (historiography) to summarize, or specific content to report on. Working in a group allows students to pool their knowledge, and it's been my observation that students are better learners when they report on their work. I have also used more on the spot 1v1 debates—asking students to argue for a particular point of view, either as an historian or person (i.e., W.E.B. DuBois vs. Booker T. Washington).

I have also employed more strategies to improve memory retention. Like the breadth of all classes at St. Andrew's, AP US History demands a lot of each student's memory. MBE science suggests that active retrieval and self-testing aid memory consolidation. As pointed out in "The Critical Importance of Retrieval for Learning,"[127] a growing body of research suggests that actively retrieving information (self-testing) produces significant long-term benefits for learning compared with passive

---

127 Karpicke, J. D. (2008). "The Critical Importance of Retrieval for Learning", *Science* 319, (February), 966–8.

studying (merely reading one's class notes or textbook). Too often, when we ask students to reflect on their study strategies, they say they simply reread class notes. Training students to build regular self-testing into their study strategies will help them embed material into their long-term memory.[128]

With the old adage "If you don't use it, you lose it" in mind (an adage now supported by research), I encourage students to study for tests and quizzes by breaking content into themes (the brain likes patterns) and repetitively trying to remember specific events, people, documents, and perspectives associated with the theme. I will also often start class asking students to spend two or three minutes to write down everything they know about a certain content area (for example—Populism). I will then ask students to share what they remembered, allowing students to add content they did not readily recall to their list.

Synthesizing history by making connections to other periods of time is another strategy I have used to aid memory and attention. I have found that linking history to current events not only expands students' horizons but makes what they are studying relevant and applicable to their lives. I can recall a particularly lively discussion about Freedmen during Reconstruction and the events in Ferguson, Missouri, in 2014. Was the failure to follow through on "40 acres and a mule" responsible for the racial divide in America today? What would America, and Ferguson, look like today had the Compromise of 1877 not taken place and racial advancement had been allowed to progress rather than thwarted for 90 years? Links such as these have resulted in some of the most interesting and engaging conversations that I have had.

Finally, I now use a greater variety of assessments to check student knowledge. Because it is an AP class, I obviously still use multiple-choice questions and essays. It is crucial that students practice these types of questions in preparation for the exam. But I mix in the occasional partner quiz or class quiz on the smartboard, or have students form a human timeline, because novelty enhances attention and motivation.

---

128 See Karpicke, J. D. and Roediger, H. L. (2008). "The Critical Importance of Retrieval for Learning." *Science*, 319(5865), 966–8; Karpicke, J. D. and Blunt, J. R. (2011). "Retrieval Practice Produces More Learning Than Elaborative Studying with Concept Mapping." *Science*, 331(6018), 772–5.

Every May, my students sit for the AP exam, which in the last year has been overhauled to reflect a move away from rote memory and towards thematic learning and historical thinking skills. As students approach the day of the exam, their stress rises, and we know from research that negative stress will ultimately create a barrier for performance. However, using the first eight months of the class to devise strategies and to find opportunities to retrieve and use information is the goal of my teaching. In the short run, students define success in this class by their score on the AP exam, and fortunately students tend to score highly on the exam. But I would also like to think that the success of this class can be measured by their passion for the subject and performance in their college history courses. The bar in AP US History is high, but I recognize that students will take many different pathways and strategies to learning the required content and skills. It is my job to make sure I offer as many research-informed strategies and pathways as possible so that all students can best learn the history and perform on the exam.

Alex Haight teaches history and is the Varsity Boys Soccer Coach at St. Andrew's.

Mathway to the Brain

At the beginning of the 21st century, there was a tremendous push in American schools, and by American parents, to get as many students started in algebra as early as possible. Maybe it was because of the results of the international PISA exam in which the United States recently finished 13 out of 39 countries in math, or because fewer college students are majoring in STEM (science, technology, engineering, and math) fields.

The St. Andrew's math department strives to have many of our graduates take the most complex math courses that we offer. But we also recognize that not all students are ready to jump into an algebra course in seventh grade. How do we find the balance to both challenge and support? All brains develop differently and have differences in learning strengths and weaknesses. However, all brains have neuroplasticity—they will develop differently based on the experiences the student has and how they unpack them. How do we best harness this neuroplasticity to grow students' ability in math?

Mind, brain, and education (MBE) science has helped the St. Andrew's math department develop research-informed answers to the questions from teachers, school leaders, and parents conscious of this national desire for growth in math.

"Math is boring," "It doesn't make sense." "When will I ever use this in my life?" These statements can sometimes be heard when students talk about math in schools. So, how does St. Andrew's get students more excited and interested in math? We know from research that when students find relevance in their academic work, as well as make a personal connection to the material, their intrinsic motivation increases. When students find the work rewarding, they are more likely to be engaged, curious, and creative. Classrooms need to connect the seemingly abstract concepts of number relationships to real-life scenarios. Teaching math concepts in isolation from their real-world application or potential career impact misses the opportunity for students to see the relevancy of their work.

Try exploring interesting math questions at the start of math class. Instead of defining prime numbers, explore the "Locker Dilemma" and have students discover number patterns in a fun way or introduce a real-life example at the beginning of each class that connects to the math concept of the day. Boredom is actually a stressor for young brains. One way to boost engagement and cut down on boredom is to include inquiry-driven projects that connect to students' interests.

How do math teachers at St. Andrew's keep students engaged? Novelty, novelty, novelty. Student engagement is a student's willingness and desire to be involved in the learning and understanding of a day's lesson. It helps motivate the students, captures their attention, and helps improve long- and short-term memory. Lessons that are stimulating, challenging, or include novelty in some way are more likely to pass through the amygdala, and the rest of the limbic system, the brain's emotional switching station, and be worked on by the prefrontal cortex and other higher-order thinking parts of the brain. Activities involving movement, humor, art, music, and competition are always welcome and often-times new to our students' daily class expectations. Arts integration has great potential to help increase student engagement and achievement. Sometimes novelty simply comes from providing students a truly awesome problem to solve. What are the novel moments in your instructional practice?

How do teachers at St. Andrew's best structure their class period? How do they begin and end class? Timing is everything according to the primacy-recency effect. The prime time to introduce new ideas or reinforce the most important information is during the first 10–12 minutes of class (assuming a 40–45 minute class period). During a learning episode, we tend to remember best that which comes first, and remember second best that which comes last. We tend to remember least that which comes just past the middle of the episode. Beginning class by just going over last night's homework might therefore be a waste of the prime time for the brain to learn new ideas. "Prime time 2" (the last 10 minutes of class) is the ideal time to summarize and reflect on the most important concepts of that day's lesson. The middle portion would be the perfect time to practice problems using the new concepts taught that day. As we all know, this structure would be difficult to maintain everyday. Often times, we do engaging activities that last an entire class period. Just being aware of this research-based class design makes lesson planning more productive.

Do students at St. Andrew's still need to memorize basic math facts? Yes, memorizing basic math facts is a crucial avenue that frees up a student's active working memory (sometimes referred to as immediate memory) so new learning can occur. Research shows that an individual can only hold 3–5 things in their active working memory.[129] If students memorize times tables, they create more space in their active working memory to conduct higher-order math. fMRI brain imaging studies show that when a student "gets" a math fact, their brain processes it in a different, more efficient way.[130] Students who have memorized math facts can focus on the complexity of higher math instead of using brain space to calculate simple equations.

How does St. Andrew's add to math's traditional trio of test, homework, and quiz to given students more feedback? Research shows that getting quality and timely feedback is crucial for learning. The main purpose of evaluation at St. Andrew's is not to assign a grade, but rather to provide students and teachers with relevant and immediate feedback about skill and knowledge acquisition so that the student can adjust learning habits and the teacher can fine-tune lesson construction. The "evaluation = chance for feedback" equation provides a fundamental shift in how the teacher perceives and constructs the class.

One quick and easy method a teacher can use is exit tickets. Before students leave class, the teacher hands out a "ticket" in which students answer a math question, define a math vocabulary word, or ask questions. Exit tickets allow teachers to check for understanding that will inform the teacher on how to construct the next day's lesson. Other forms of feedback

129 Cowan, N. (2008). "What Are the Differences between Long-Term, Short-Term, and Working Memory?" *Progress in Brain Research*, 169, 323–8.
130 Dr. Jay Giedd. (2010). Personal communication.

that we recommend include practice assessments, written reflections, student-made assessments, ungraded (formative) pop quizzes, warm-ups and "Do Nows". Switching the traditional pop quiz to frequent no-stakes or low-stakes formative assessments is a particularly good change, as it allows students to assess where they are with their understanding and teachers to assess what further work they need to do to prepare students.

We have recently adopted the idea of "deliberate difficulty" into our teaching. Studies suggest that if learning is difficult, although retrieval strength may be weaker in the short term, in the long term it will be stronger. When we create practice assessments, which the students request all the time, we purposely make them more difficult and challenging than the actual test, quiz, or assignment. "A teacher's job is not to make work easy. It is to make it difficult. If you are not challenged, you do not make mistakes. If you do not make mistakes, feedback is useless." Finally, no matter how challenging it seems, providing immediate feedback is crucial and particularly important in math. The mere anticipation of rapid feedback even helps—studies suggest that students who know they will receive feedback sooner tend to perform better than those who know they will receive grades after a greater delay.

The flipped classroom seems to be the talk in educational practices. What are St. Andrew's thoughts? The flipped classroom has generated a lot of interest and conversation in education recently especially because of the work of Khan Academy and LearnZillon. The idea is for students to watch video lectures at home, and then do the "homework" in class with the teacher and their classmates discussing the assignments. Watching videos on their own allows students to pause and re-watch the lesson if they need to study a problem or need something repeated. We have used the flipped classroom with a few select units in a precalculus course. Some students found this method very helpful, while others had a hard time adjusting to this new way of teaching.

Research tells us that all students have learning differences—things they are currently good at and things they currently are not so good at. It is no surprise, therefore, that the flipped classroom might help some students but not others. Research on multiple intelligences and learning differences tells us that the teacher should select methods to teach and assess based on the content they want to teach.[131] Trying to teach to an individual student's preferred learning style is a neuromyth proven false by research. It is one of the most common neuromyths that incorrectly informs instructional decisions.[132] Thus, some topics will be best taught by the flipped classroom method, others in a more traditional, teacher-directed, setting. The expert teacher, by deeply knowing the essential representations and questions of their subject, figures out which, and does so taking feedback from their class and the variety of experiences they have recently had into consideration.

The most important change, however, is the professional development mindset of the math department. Collaborative, research–informed reflective practice is key. Based on research, your own experience and expertise, and discussions with colleagues, try something out. Evaluate how it works, tweak it, and try again. With this iterative mindset, we are better than we were last year, and next year we will be better still.

---

131 See: Dr. Mariale Hardiman and Glenn Whitman's "Assessment and the Learning Brain." Independent School (Winter 2014), www.thecttl.org.

132 Garnder, H. and Reigeluth, C. M. (eds.). (1999). *Instructional-Design Theories and Models: A New Paradigm of Instructional Theory* (1st edition, Volume II). Lawrence Erlbaum Associates.

Judy Kee teaches math and science and is the Co-Head of the Lower School at St. Andrew's. Gregg Ponitch teaches math and is the assistant coach for the boys varsity soccer team at St. Andrew's.

Using Creative Writing to Improve Memory

As English teachers, we often use analytical writing assignments to assess reading comprehension and understanding. However, one underutilized method for engaging with text is creative writing. English teachers have been using close reading and passage analysis for years to highlight important moments in stories and to help students dig into word choice to produce a concise, formal written analysis. But what happens when a student tries to put herself or himself into a character's metaphorical shoes?

Engaging in this type of creative writing task changes the exercise from an external literary analysis to an internal view of a character's feelings and emotions. One goal of the creative writing exercise—and reading in general—is to create empathy and develop students' theory of mind, which involves understanding why someone acts in a particular way or predicting how someone will act.[133] Empathy and theory of mind are both central to social cognition, and researchers have determined that character-driven stories consistently lead to the synthesis of oxytocin, a hormone that motivates cooperation with others by strengthening one's sense of empathy.[134]

---

133 Thompson, B. N. (2017). "Theory of Mind: Understanding Others in a Social World." *Psychology Today*, 3 July, https://www.psychologytoday.com/blog/socioemotional-success/201707/theory-mind-understanding-others-in-social-world/.

134 Zak, P. J. (2013). "How Stories Change the Brain." *Greater Good Magazine*, 17 December, https://greatergood.berkeley.edu/article/item/how_stories_change_brain.

In addition to enhanced social cognition, an important outcome of this creative writing task is the improvement of memory. Using stories to learn activates the brain's positive emotional state and transfers the information more readily into memory.[135] For students with strong memory or those who love the story, remembering events and scenes may not be that difficult. But what about students who do not necessarily connect with the storyline or characters? What could help them remember key scenes? To answer this question, we asked our students to engage in the exercise of writing from the perspective of another character.

An fMRI study found that when participants continued to write creatively from a literary text that was given to them, the areas of their brain at work were those involving language processing, working memory, and the long-term memory system.[136] We saw this impact firsthand; while engaged in this creative writing task, students juggled a myriad of cognitive tasks, including remembering plot details, character traits, common language used by the character, and the context of the scene students were asked to re-create.

When students in English 8 were asked to choose a character from the jail scene in "To Kill a Mockingbird," the scene in which Atticus is guarding Tom Robinson from racist farmers who want him dead, students chose a range of perspectives. They had to play with words and sentence structures; they were even allowed to break traditional grammar rules for the sake of artistic license. One English 8 student wrote the following from Atticus Finch's perspective:

"My mouth is frozen open, my fists clenched tightly, and my heart still beating way too fast. Scout's voice wrenches at something inside of me and I look away from Jem, who stands in front of me with his own fists clenched at his sides. He has my eyes... A prideful voice whispers inside of me as I turn to look at my daughter, he has my hair too... As my gaze lands on Scout, my heart slows its anxious thrum."

135 Willis, J. (2017). "The Neuroscience of Narrative and Memory," 12 September, Edutopia, https://www.edutopia.org/article/neuroscience-narrative-and-memory.
136 Shah, C., Erhard, K., Ortheil, H.-J., Kaza, E., Kessler, C. and Lotze, M. (2013). "Neural Correlates of Creative Writing: An fMRI Study." *Human Brain Mapping*, 34(5), 1088–101.

When a student creates and writes like the above character, she/he is an author too. Thinking about which words to choose and which feelings to evoke creates a deeper connection to the moment and, therefore, creates a stronger memory of the plot and characters. Recreating this particular scene from Atticus's perspective could have even more lasting effects, as studies have found that when students discover meaning in characters' good deeds, they are often motivated to act more virtuously as well.[137]

We asked our 11th grade students to do the same creative writing exercise for our unit on *The Great Gatsby*. Incorporating more choice for our older students, we asked them to pick from a select number of scenes in addition to choosing the character whose perspective they wanted adopt. Some students not only used language common to the character, but also incorporated literary devices such as foreshadowing and irony. For example, one student wrote from the perspective of Myrtle Wilson shortly before she dies:

"She looks so out of place. I should be sitting next to him, not her. But that car is so... It's unforgettable. That car is something else. If I was in that car, I would leave quite an impression on anyone who should look. It definitely will leave an impression on me."

The benefits of this assignment multiply when you ask students to read their work aloud so that they can appreciate each other's creativity and remember the scenes and emotions of the characters more clearly. When reading, hearing, and writing stories, our brains are wired to focus on the characters' thoughts and feelings[138]—if stories are memorable, it is because of the people within them. If students can connect to characters, they can more easily learn from them, choosing which qualities they want to avoid and which they want to emulate. Creative writing that incorporates choice, empathy, and memory empowers students to become authors, both of the story they are rewriting and of their own life stories.

---

137 Gotlieb, R., Jahner, E. E., Immordino-Yang, M. H. and Kaufman, S. B. (2015). "How Social-Emotional Imagination Facilitates Deep Learning and Creativity in the Classroom." In R. A. Beghetto & J. C. Kaufman (eds.). *Nuturing Creativity in the Classroom* (2nd edition). Cambridge Press.

138 Yuan, Y., Major-Girardin, J. and Brown, S. (2018). "Storytelling Is Intrinsically Mentalistic: A Functional Magnetic Resonance Imaging Study of Narrative Production across Modalities." *Journal of Cognitive Neuroscience*, 30(9), 1298–314.

Liz Regan Kiingi teaches English at St. Andrew's. Julia Dean was the CTTL Academy Program Coordinator and Innovation Associate and English teacher at St. Andrew's during the writing of this research-informed article.

Making It Stick Better

Much of the memory research in this piece is taken from Peter Brown, Mark McDaniel, and Henry Roediger III's *Make It Stick: The Science of Successful Learning*.

Biology and history. Two high school courses that seem very disparate from one another. One is all about microscopes and critters while the other is all about dates and battles. Or at least that's what conventional wisdom would have you believe. But when teachers at St. Andrew's consider these courses, we find that we have more in common than you might think. While the subject matter is very different, a common thread between them is memory. How can we help students learn the facts and concepts that exist in each course both for and beyond the summative test or project?

We can think of memory as creating pegs in our students' brains on which they hang the specific pieces of information that they read or discover. The real trick is for the students to retrieve what they have learned; in fact, the human brain can easily learn a lot of material very quickly—it's the retrieval that's so challenging. So, how do we help our students become more capable retrievers? For us it began by looking at the research, in particular, *Make It Stick: The Science of Successful Learning*. Memory, like all brain functions, is not isolated to one region of the brain—and without it, learning does not happen. What follows is how we have translated research on memory to our respective disciplines, both at the advanced placement and non-AP levels.

Illusion of Learning: For years we promised students that if they would just review their active reading highlights or notes, they would succeed and demonstrate mastery. But research shows how misguided that is because familiarity with material tends to result in the illusion that you have learned it. Research shows that when students must pull information out of their brains, they remember material better than if they re-read the information. So now in biology, our students interact with the material to make it stick better. They build electronic flashcards using Quizlet for vocabulary recall, orally explain diagrams to their family members, quiz each other, rewrite their notes in a novel format, or use their notes packet to generate review sheets. Such strategies cross-over into history as well. Students in history class "self-test" by writing out essential names, dates, and ideas on a blank sheet of paper without any reference to their books or notes so that they can see how much they remember. Then they go back with their text open to fill in the gaps. These active retrieval strategies that are designed to be "deliberately difficult" are so much more than simply, and passively, "looking over their notes."

Priming the Brain for Learning: Research shows that when students try to pull information from their brain before they learn it, they will remember it better when they have learned it. For example, students were asked "What made the French Revolution revolutionary?" before they had read the chapter. They had to generate information about the movements leading up to the French Revolution, based on their prior knowledge, and predict why it was such a game changer. Even if they got the wrong answers, which they probably should, having not studied the French Revolution very much, they were priming their brains to be aware of incoming information. In biology class, students are asked to predict what will happen next, be it in a metabolic pathway diagram or by predicting the effect of doubling the volume of yeast in a fermentation experiment. All of these in-class strategies keep students engaged in the learning process and have been shown to help our students retain what we want them to remember better.

Assessment: Research shows that frequent low-stakes or no stakes formative assessments help students recall information more effectively than almost any other study technique. After learning about DNA replication, for example, students close their notes and take a three-question mini-quiz on what they just learned. Or on Fridays we might have a quiz that could be on any material we have studied so far this year. Since the stakes are low, wrong answers simply alert a student that she or he needs to focus more on that area, but the grade does not torpedo a student's average. It also alerts us to where we might need to focus additional teaching. Research shows that better learning happens when students frequently engage in low-stakes quizzing because they have a better sense of what they know and don't know due to the retrieval practice. Also, the act of retrieval helps students memorize the material for future use, with multiple "spaced" attempts at this helping even more.

Success Stories: In biology, students spend considerable time learning about various phyla (groups) of animals in the animal kingdom. A lot of vocabulary and a lack of familiarity with the huge variety of living creatures in the world makes this a difficult topic for ninth graders. To help students keep their memory pegs clean and connected, they are encouraged to make concept maps for review. They are provided with vocabulary words in large type. Students cut these out and arrange them to reflect terms and concepts that are unique to each animal group, and then tape them onto large sheets of construction paper in a way that makes sense to them. Finally, they write in definitions, additional terms or ideas, and helpful memory tips. The whole process IS their review, and what they create is essentially a review sheet. In fact, a student really won't learn well from just looking at another student's concept map—it's the making of the map that helps a student figure out what they know and what they still need to learn. The first student who did this many years ago went from earning a C on tests to earning As.

In history, research recommends manipulating course content out of sequence in some way in order to "make it stick." My first action was to try to attack the summer reading in that way; students had read the first volume of the *Norton History of Modern Europe on the Renaissance and Reformation*. Students were assigned a country and had to follow that country throughout the book and tell the story of that country in the period of the Renaissance and Reformation.

The next step was to have students create an actual timeline that runs around the walls of our classroom. The country that the students had been assigned for their presentation on the summer reading was the country they would have to represent on the timeline. They came up with the idea of each country being a separate color. The timeline serves a multitude of purposes. Ideally, when they are taking the AP exam they will be able to shut their eyes and imagine where events are on the timeline. Having each country be a different color allows for students to see patterns on the timeline and, again, see and speak the narrative of that country. Finally, the action of deciding what goes on the timeline gives rise to great conversation and thinking. By associating a memory with a specific place in the room, students were creating memory palaces they could use to store this information. The novelty, choice, and personal buy-in of this activity also deepened student engagement, which aided their learning.

The Teacher Researcher: Students get the novel experience of watching us be happily immersed doing something we routinely ask them to do—research. This is a topic fundamental to both our subjects. In our work on memory, as good researchers do, we try something, observe, reflect on what worked and what didn't, tweak things, and try again. We model good research practice with, in front of, and for our students.

Conclusion: What's our take-away message? We intentionally apply research about memory in our classroom teaching. In addition, we share it with the students so that they can use those strategies to retrieve information and be more successful. Students in AP european history or biology may never take another western civilization or life science course in their lives, but it's our goal that they remember these classes and what they learned about the world around them. Applying this research is a winning strategy for teachers on a more personal level as well. Why did we get into this profession? We love working with young people, but we also love our content and crave the opportunity to share the big ideas and the details. Translating educational neuroscience into the classroom gives us more opportunities to share our passions in a real and lasting way with our students.

We all win.

Amanda Freeman, who has since retired, taught history at St. Andrew's.

Phyllis Robinson, who has since retired, taught biology at St. Andrew's and was a CTTL/Omidyar Teacher Research Fellow and Neuroteach Global Mission grader.

The Use of Laboratory Exercises as Formative Experiences in the Science Classroom

"I'm bad at science." Those dreaded words are some of the most demotivating to a science teacher. What have I done to make them believe that they don't belong in science? How is it possible for someone to be "bad" at it?

Science is, and always will be, about discovery through failure. It is such a pivotal element of the subject that we routinely conduct error analyses in real-world laboratories with the expectation that hypotheses *will* fail. P-values under a measly 5% are the only ones considered statistically significant; anything else is rejected outright. That's a low bar for failure!

So then why does it feel like so many students grapple with their sense of belonging in the subject? It is my opinion that teachers (myself included) have gotten caught in the cycle of grading laboratory exercises based on accuracy and not on process. In doing so, we are punishing students for the very thing that spawned the majority of major scientific discoveries. What if we reimagined laboratory exercises so that the process of science, and idea of failing productively, are at their heart?

THE (MISALIGNED) PURPOSES OF LABORATORY EXERCISES
Traditionally, labs are run in science classrooms for two purposes. The first is to provide a practical application of content knowledge in order

to further cement understanding of learning objectives. The second is to gauge student achievement by assessing that understanding.

These purposes are both valid and reasonable. The issue is not with the first purpose of the laboratory, as it's what makes science one of the most inherently fun subjects (when else can you make something explode in the name of learning?). It is the latter purpose that is troubling, not because labs *shouldn't* be used to gauge student achievement but the manner in which teachers often do so.

When we grade labs based on accuracy regarding concepts that students have only just begun to explore, we are setting them up for failure. As teachers, we have *experience* to lean on to provide us with perspective on that failure. We project that experience upon our students, expecting them to understand, despite them not having the same experiences as we have. And yet we are continually surprised that when we punish them for their failures with a grade, and then tell them that failure is "natural," students equate their own failure with "I'm bad at science." If failure is natural, then they must be *naturally bad at it*. We know from research that experts and novices learn differently[139] and we should design laboratory exercises with this in mind.

LABORATORY EXERCISES AS FORMATIVE ASSESSMENT

Formative assessments are the ultimate scientific endeavor for teachers. A teacher conducts an experiment to collect data. They are testing their results against a null hypothesis: that no learning has occurred. Based on the results of their experiment, teachers either prove or disprove the null hypothesis via statistics, either with actual data or with anecdotal evidence.

Labs should be assessed in this way for two main reasons. The first is that it more accurately mirrors real-world laboratory endeavors: scientists aren't assessed on whether they get the "right" answers or not (in reality, there are none in real labs), they're assessed on *what answers they were able to achieve*. The second is that sometimes executive functioning and basic laboratory skills can get in the way of

139 Kirschner, P. and Hendrick, C. (2020). *How Learning Happens: Seminal Works in Educational Psychology and What They Mean in Practice*. Routledge.

achieving "right" answers, which is not necessarily indicative of a lack of understanding.

So then what purpose do labs serve if not to formally assess student knowledge?

LABORATORY EXERCISES AS LEARNING EXPERIENCES

A student should not be blamed for not being able to perform on a laboratory exercise based on knowledge they have only just acquired. They are still in the middle of the process of learning that material. This is what *formative* assessments are for: they provide students with a snapshot of their current understanding and feedback on what they need to do to improve. As Stuart Firestein writes in his book *Failure: Why Science Is So Successful*, "Failures provide a certain kind of feedback that is then used in a process we call error correction. With this simple loop in place, knowing that something doesn't work can be as valuable as knowing that it does."[140] This needs to be a fundamental part of student labs.

Labs are *learning experiences*, where students should be able to connect the dots between the data that they are collecting and the content that they are learning. If they can't, it's because of two reasons: (1) the lab was poorly designed or (2) they don't have an appropriate depth of knowledge yet.

Neither of these reasons are the students' fault. While the former is a valuable insight for the teacher to help them refine their practice, the latter is an exciting opportunity for the class. It means that the student realizes that they don't know a critical content element but aren't being punished for it. It also means that the teacher realizes this same thing and can then guide students appropriately to understanding. Students can then be permitted to "try again" with no consequences. Failure becomes "normal," as it should, but also accepted as a means to an end rather than simply an "end." It also more faithfully mirrors the process of real-world science.

---

140 Firestein, S. (2015). *Failure: Why Science Is So Successful*. Oxford University Press.

BELONGING IN SCIENCE

How does this strategy impact a student's sense of belonging in science?

If grades don't matter in the lab anymore, why shouldn't labs become collaborative endeavors where one student's perspective can uplift the collective? Capitalizing on students' varying zones of proximal development can allow for a diverse range of perspectives on achieved data. This sharing of knowledge has no negative impact on students; their grades are not at stake here. What is at stake is whether discovery gets to continue! Students want to know more about science because it provides an understanding of their world, but understanding only comes when students feel equipped to handle it. Diverse perspectives via collaborative data analysis can do that. Furthermore, we need to design scaffolded opportunities for this to happen into the laboratory experiences we create and not just leave it to chance.

Even deeper, though, is that normalizing failure in the lab by detaching grades from it opens science to everyone. It is no longer an elite bastion where only right answers are celebrated. Everyone's experience and perspective suddenly matters, because the lab becomes a realm of learning where sharing both successes *and* failures are integral to understanding. In other words, *any* data-driven answer becomes a "right" answer.

And that's how science *should* be.

Ryan Marklewitz teaches science at St. Andrew's, where he also coaches cross country, track, and swimming.

The Science of Forgetting and the Art of Remembering (Part I)

Have we learned this before? Few student inquiries are more unnerving for a teacher distributing a final exam review packet at the end of an ostensibly successful year than this one. Calmly, we state, "Yes, we studied that earlier in the year!" and instinctively hide our exasperation and disappointment. We are frustrated at ourselves for failing to help our students learn and disappointed that even given our best efforts many of our students perfected the science of forgetting more skillfully than the art of remembering.

As professional educators, we know our role is to promote learning and not just cover curriculum. However, few of us are righteous enough to say that fostering learning is not in perpetual conflict with the need (artificial or real) to cover a prescribed curriculum.

Even when we enthusiastically infuse our classes with hands-on activities, group work, purposeful connections, and multi-media delivery, the result is more often than not a chapter by chapter, linear presentation of topics that will produce the dreaded year-end question: "Have we learned this before?"

In the late 1800s, Hermann Ebbinghaus, a German psychologist, became known for his research on memory retrieval, aptly named the "forgetting curve." Ebbinghaus's forgetting curve has the shape of a decreasing exponential function, which is disturbing to a math teacher because the greatest rate of decline in memory, i.e., the steepest portion of the curve, occurs within the first few hours or days of learning a new topic. All students, even high achieving, highly motivated ones, forget huge swathes of what they learned. For example, Eugène Custers found that medical students forget 30% of basic science facts in one year, and over 50% in two.[141] How can we improve this?

From his research, Ebbinghaus determined that an individual's ability to retain information is dependent on two main factors: the strength or durability of the memory and the amount of time passed since learning it. Strength or durability of memory is a complex attribute associated with individual relevance, connection, and the use of memory representation like a mnemonic device. This aspect of learning is one that educators focus on naturally. Making content relevant, helping students make connections, and providing study strategies like mnemonic devices are the cornerstones of excellent teaching.[142]

The effect of elapsed time on retention is a feature of learning that teachers pay less attention to, even though the amount of research on it is large, robust, and compelling. Ebbinghaus, along with many researchers since then,[143, 144] confirmed that retention is dramatically improved when material is relearned at spaced intervals. Spaced repetitions—forcing ourselves to recall information just as we are beginning to forget it—serve as reminders that bolster memory and have the effect of flattening out the forgetting curve. The graph below shows a flattening of the forgetting curve with each repetition or review of material.

We keep the spacing effect in mind as we plan each unit of study leading up to a summative assessment, creating a rhythm that helps students

---

141 Custers, E. (2010). "Long-Term Retention of Basic Science Knowledge: A Review Study." *Advances in Health Science Education: Theory & Practice*, 15(1), 109–28.

142 Brown, P. C., Roediger III, H. L. and McDaniel, M. A. (2014). *Make It Stick: The Science of Successful Learning*. Belknap Press.

143 Dunlosky, J., Rawson, K., Marsh, E., Nathan, M. and Willingham, D. (2013). "Improving Students' Learning with Effective Learning Techniques: Promising Directions from Cognitive and Educational Psychology." *Psychological Science in the Public Interest*, 14(1) 4–58.

144 Pashler, H., Bain, P., Bottge, B., Graesser, A., Koedinger, K., McDaniel, M. and Metcalfe, J. (2007). "Organizing Instruction and Study to Improve Student Learning" (NCER 2007-2004). National Center for Education Research, Institute of Education Sciences, US Department of Education.

learn the material. But what if we applied the spacing effect throughout an entire year-long course? What would that look like? This is called interleaving. Instead of going linearly through each unit, we revisit topics again and again just as students begin to forget the material. This seems like the optimum way to plan a course in a way that is designed to make it stick in students' minds.

However, interleaving isn't the norm in most classroom environments. First, our course materials, presented chapter-by-chapter, don't lend themselves to interleaving. Second, as educators, it seems unnatural to leave a topic before students have mastered it, and mastery typically culminates in a large unit assessment for which the vast majority of students will cram. The forgetting curve demonstrates that cramming, or trying to remember vast material in one study session, is the least effective method for learning. It should come as no surprise then that a year of linearly presented topics with few opportunities to review, revisit, and relearn material at spaced intervals results in that dreaded student question: "Have we learned this before?"[145]

Armed with this research and weary of the influence of the forgetting curve on our students, a colleague and I decided to overhaul our Algebra 2/Trigonometry curriculum during the 2016–2017 school year. We began by deconstructing the entire course. We created a list of overarching topics that we wanted the students to master, and, using large flash cards, we taped each of these topics across a whiteboard in the front of a classroom. We spent hours ordering and reordering these topics until we were comfortable that each topic connected logically to the next. Under each topic we listed subtopics based on their ability and relevance to support what we wanted the students to learn. The textbook, websites, and other online materials were used as secondary resources.

To interleave our curriculum, we designed homework that included ideas presented in prior units and assessed a topic only after students had multiple opportunities to practice it. We provided weekly graded algebra review worksheets that continually reinforced prior content. Interleaving

---

145 Akresh-Gonzales, J. (2019). "Spaced Repetition: The Most Effective Way to Learn." *NEJM Knowledge*, 17 May, https://knowledgeplus.nejm.org/blog/spaced-repetition-the-most-effective-way-to-learn/.

required significant planning and detailed calendaring. A calendar for a week could include teaching geometric series, giving homework on exponential functions, and preparing students for a quiz or test on a unit learned the prior month.

Fast forward to the end of the year. The day arrives to distribute final exam review packets. We distribute the packets and instruct students to preview them. We wait for the dreaded question that never came. The students begin working. Not even one student asked, "Have we learned this before?"

So, was interleaving successful? It is difficult to know for sure. We can say that final exam preparation seemed to be significantly less stressful for the students than in prior years, and that there were few "very poor" exam grades. Written feedback solicited from students at the end of the exam indicated that they felt well-prepared and thought the exam was fair. So, where will these students be on the forgetting curve in the fall when they arrive to their precalculus class, a course that is completely dependent on material learned in Algebra 2/Trigonometry? As luck would have it, I am teaching precalculus next year. Stay tuned...

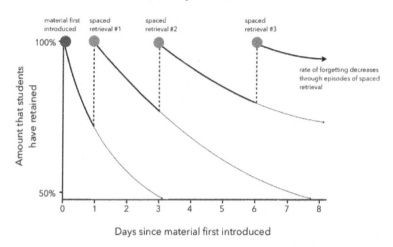

'Forgetting Curve' showing the effect of spaced retrieval

material first introduced — spaced retrieval #1 — spaced retrieval #2 — spaced retrieval #3

rate of forgetting decreases through episodes of spaced retrieval

Amount that students have retained

Days since material first introduced

How long should you wait between episodes of spaced retrieval? A good rule of thumb is wait until students are just forgetting it.

Traditional sequence of massed units

Unit 1   Unit 2   Unit 3   Unit 4   Unit 5   Unit 6

Interleaved units

Unit 1   Unit 2   Unit 3   Unit 4   Unit 5   Unit 6

Karen Kaufman teaches math at St. Andrew's and was the head of the math department during the writing of this article.

The Science of Forgetting and the Art of Remembering (Part II)

"Have we learned this before?" is one of the most unsettling questions a teacher can hear from students at the end of what was thought to be a successful school year. It is also the first line of an article I wrote in 2017 for Volume 3 of the CTTL's *Think Differently and Deeply* publication. This article, "The Science of Forgetting and The Art of Remembering," described how a colleague and I implemented spaced repetition and interleaving in our Algebra 2/Trigonometry classes.

If you are thinking, hold on, topics in math courses don't lend themselves to spacing and interleaving, you are right. But this might be because you are thinking of the math classroom you are used to. Traditionally, math topics are presented linearly, each building on the prior one—envision a textbook's table of contents that a class spends the year working through. However, I was at a point in my teaching career when I could no longer deny the dissatisfaction that students and I both felt at the end of a school year when it was time to prepare for the final exam.

Student stress and lower-than-anticipated final exam grades had become an expected end of year norm. The final exam seemed to be a measurement of how well students crammed for the exam rather than how well they had learned throughout the year. And, our math teachers were spending the better part of each new school year revisiting prior year's content to make up for students forgetting much of what they had learned.

Since math is a subject that continues to build on prior knowledge, this was a debilitating cycle for all involved. What's more frustrating is that we knew why the forgetting was happening. As research-informed educators, we were familiar with Hermann Ebbinghaus's study of memory retrieval aptly named the "forgetting curve." The forgetting curve has the shape of a decreasing exponential-like function with the greatest decline in memory (steepest portion of the curve) occurring within the first few hours or days of learning a new topic. The antidote to forgetting was to revisit the topics at appropriately-spaced intervals.

So, after years of frustration, and armed with this compelling research, my brave colleague and I decided to try spacing and interleaving. We completely deconstructed and reorganized our Algebra 2/Trigonometry course to provide ongoing and multiple opportunities for student exposure to new content. We abandoned the linearly presented order of topics in our textbook and instead connected subtopics based on their relation to other subtopics.

We peppered topics strategically and repeatedly throughout the course. To fully establish interleaving and spacing, we chose to lag all homework by establishing a weekly homework review sheet. Homework was assigned based on ideas presented in prior units. A topic would never appear on a weekly homework review until it had been practiced extensively and repeatedly in class. Assessments were also lagged often several weeks after a topic was first taught and after students had multiple practice opportunities.

At the end of my 2017 article, I promised to update readers on the outcome of this new pedagogy. As a math teacher and numbers person, the plan was to collect quantitative data on student final exam grades (in precalculus) from year to year to determine if students coming from Algebra 2/Trigonometry were forgetting less. We collected and analyzed the data and found that final exam scores were in fact somewhat higher since we implemented spacing and interleaving. However, these outcomes can't be relied on as statistically significant since the composition of students in our classes vary from year to year. In this past year, there was an unusually large contingent of precalculus students who came from Honors Algebra 2/Trigonometry. Therefore, it is unreasonable to state definitively that the increase in exam scores was related to our new methods.

It turns out, perhaps the most compelling data to support spacing and interleaving is not quantitative at all. Instead, it is the qualitative feedback from students and teachers. Students who experienced spaced repetition and interleaving in their math classrooms were happier and less stressed throughout the school year and especially during the final exam period. We know from a 2014 research study on happiness by the CTTL and Research Schools International that there is a statistically significant correlation between happiness and students' GPA from elementary school through high school.[146]

One of our goals then as math teachers should be to generate happier more confident math students. In that regard, I do believe the data is compelling. This past year, four of our math courses adopted spacing and interleaving. At the end of the year, we surveyed students asking them specifically what they thought about their weekly review homework, and the interleaving of course content. Student feedback was overwhelmingly positive and only a few students surveyed said that they preferred a more traditional approach to learning and homework. Here's a small sampling of student feedback:

"I really like the weekly review homework because it helps me quickly figure out what I know and what I don't, and then I can get help with the things I don't know and carry those skills over to the next assignment."

"I really like the review homework because I feel like I am not reaching for help every time we encounter something older in class or during practice. It keeps me actively thinking about concepts that in other subjects, we would forget about in the next year after the summer. It allows me to manage my time better as well because I can space out the time I will need to complete it and work on homework when I have the time. As stated before, I truly feel like I benefit from this system more than previous ones."

Beginning in the 2019–2020 school year, all of our middle and upper school math courses will adopt some form of spacing and interleaving. And we will design an improved action-research study to measure the impact. Over the coming years, we will continue to observe and report on the effects of this new pedagogy on student learning, particularly on retention from year to year, and on student attitudes toward math. Stay tuned... again.

---

146 "Because I'm Happy." Harvard Graduate School of Education, https://www.gse. harvard.edu/news/uk/15/03/because-i%E2%80%99m-happy.

'Forgetting Curve' showing the effect of spaced retrieval

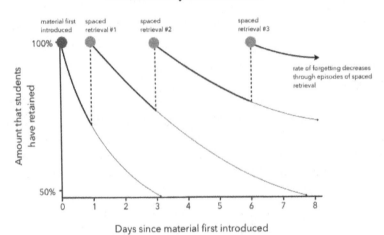

Days since material first introduced

How long should you wait between episodes of spaced retrieval? A good rule of thumb is wait until students are just forgetting it.

Karen Kaufman teaches math at St. Andrew's and was the head of the math department during the writing of this article.

Dialing Down Stress without Dumbing Down My Class

At St. Andrew's, we are living through year two of our new daily schedule (see *Think Differently & Deeply*, Volume 3), designed to deepen learning and support student well-being. It is based on the fundamental principle that deep academic challenge and well-being are intertwined—that great schools design for both, rather than force students and parents to make a false choice. The flow of each day and the school week as a whole has been a revelation. But this got me thinking: changing a schedule is a large-scale effort. What was I doing on a smaller scale in my physics class to combine rigor and well-being, strategies that could be done by any teacher without asking permission? Here are just a few:

DISRUPTING THE RHYTHM

When I started teaching I fell into a familiar rhythm, like the beat of a dance track: quiz, quiz, quiz, test, quiz, quiz, quiz, test... Everything counted. But a light went off while in a conversation with a colleague who said, "Sean is so good on tests; it is a shame his quiz grades are so low, they are really dragging his grade down." It was a revelation—surely his test grade was by far the most important measure of what Sean ultimately knew, and if he failed the quizzes but ultimately learned from them, why should the quizzes count against him?

FORMATIVE ASSESSMENTS

And then I learned about formative assessments. One of the most dramatic changes since I have started using research to inform my teaching has been knowledge and impact of formative assessments. They are a low- or no-stakes tool to find out what students currently know and can do, and what they are still struggling with. And then, importantly, I can alter my teaching based on what I find out, and get students to alter their practicing and studying based on what they find out. I made the commitment to never put a concept, skill, or block of key knowledge on a test that students had not previously encountered on a formative assessment. This commitment made me change the way I design my day-to-day teaching to make it happen. I also talk to my students about what formative assessment is, why we are doing it, and how we are shifting things about a bit in my course based on what we find out. On occasion I move a test when it is clear my students are not ready.

I used to think that if I felt I had done an awesome job teaching, my students must be ready for that test. I now realize that just because I may have walked out of my classroom feeling that, wow, my teaching was awesome today, it doesn't mean the learning I wanted to happen had actually happened. Formative assessment is the way to find out.[147] Including regular formative assessment and a regular dialogue about it with my class has lessened the stress level around major assessments, as students know where they are and have an opportunity to act while there is still time. Without quizzes I have fewer grades in my grade book, so in essence each test counts for more, but the stress level is down because students feel better prepared for the test. There appears to be no negative impact on grades, and it seems to actually help some students.

TEACH STRATEGIES ALONGSIDE CONTENT

I used to believe that my job was to teach content. By the time students reached me they had a good toolbox of skills, now it was up to me to deliver chemistry and physics. I now know from research that most students, left to their own devices, use ineffective or inefficient study strategies, like rereading the textbook with lots of highlighters. I also know that

---

147 Wiliam, D. (2018). *Embedded Formative Assessment*. Solution Tree Press.

students' ability to carry over skills that work in one class to another, or from one year to another, tends to be much less than we appreciate, and they benefit from an intentional academic nudge to use their prior knowledge and skills on current tasks.[148] So now I teach study strategies alongside content, particularly active retrieval and spaced practice.[149]

Active retrieval is the idea that self-testing is much more effective for long-term memory storage and retrieval than passively reading. Spacing is the idea of allowing students some time to get a bit rusty before making them recall information or skills that they are just starting to forget. I design the content and schedule of my homework with active retrieval and spaced practice in mind. The goal of most of my homework is to get students ready for assessments through a planned sequence of just-forgetting, forcing yourself to recall, then checking in with your notes or with me when you cannot. This is another part of helping reduce students' stress level for assessments by making them feel better prepared, and by increasing their confidence that they have a great toolbox of strategies to draw on.

ACKNOWLEDGE LIMITED WORKING MEMORY

I used to think that being able to hold 20 things in your brain at once was part of learning science. Some people could do it, others could not; this was just part of the process of figuring out if science was for you. I now appreciate that working memory and higher-order thinking are separate things. Related, yes, but particularly in the novice stage of learning the core knowledge and skills in a new subject, working memory capacity can be a real barrier.[150] You are asked to hold so many things in your working memory at once that you do not have the capacity to do the task. Or you can do the task now, but do not have the capacity to commit it to long-term memory so you can do it later. So now I build knowledge step-

---

148 Quigley, A., Muijs, D. and Stringer, E. (2018). *Metacognition and Self-Regulated Learning, Guidance Report.* Education Endowment Foundation.

149 Pashler, H., Bain, P. M., Bottge, B. A., Graesser, A. C., Koedinger, K. R., McDaniel, M. A. and Metcalfe, J. (2007). *Organizing Instruction and Study to Improve Student Learning, IES Practice Guide.* National Center for Education Research.

150 van Merrienboer, J. J. G., Kirschner, P. A. and Kester, L. (2003). "Taking the Load Off a Learner's Mind: Instructional Design for Complex Learning." *Educational Psychologist*, 38(1), 5–13.

by-purposeful-step, lessening the demands on students' active working memory because key skills and knowledge for the learning now had already been stored in long-term memory earlier. It feels easier to students because of this. I also add in simple scaffolds to reduce the cognitive load at times, such as providing worked examples for homework in the early stages of learning a new skill, or allowing students to use a sheet of equations when we start a new unit. These scaffolds will get peeled away over time as students' confidence and competence grow, but they lessen stress when students are in the "novice" stage of a new topic.

There is, of course, much more, and it evolves constantly. Once the idea is fixed in your mind that well-being and academic challenge go hand in hand, it becomes a part of your daily lesson planning. Some degree of stress helps learning, but lots does not—so as a teacher I am constantly a stress balancer. We might think of this as a two-pronged approach to well-being that includes strategies for instruction and assessment, and social-emotional strategies, some of which are shown in the table below. By designing for the well-being of my students I am also building my capacity to get them to think harder and dig deeper. Yes, as a school we can do that through large-scale projects like a daily schedule. But as a teacher, I can do it every day too.

Dr. Ian Kelleher teaches science at St. Andrew's, is the Dreyfuss Family Chair of Research for the Center of Transformative Teaching and Learning, and is co-author of the book *Neuroteach: Brain Science and the Future of Education.*

A two-pronged approach to well-being (includes, but is not limited to...)

Instruction and assessment	Social-emotional
Teach memory strategies alongside content	Belonging mindset & identity formation
Be deliberate about metacognition	Growth mindset
Teach and assess in multiple modalities	Purpose and relevance
Use formative assessment	Metacognition about stress
Use research on what good feedback looks like	The language a teacher uses
Curriculum design (interleaving & cognitive load)	The importance of relationships

This article title was created by Standford University's Graduate School of Education professor Dr. Denise Pope for a workshop that Denise and Ian co-presented at SXSW EDU2019.

On Pilgrimage in the Classroom

Teaching is like a pilgrimage—each term has its own destination and travel companions in students and colleagues. In the summer of 2018, my colleague Chantal Cassan-Moudoud and I were presented with the opportunity to complete an actual pilgrimage through St. Andrew's Summer Grants Program. Our journey was to Santiago de Compostela, located in the northeast corner of Spain.

The Camino de Santiago, or the Way of St. James, began in the Middle Ages. Tradition tells us that the Apostle James was sent to evangelize the Iberian Peninsula and was later buried in Compostela after being martyred in the Holy Land. Eventually, a cathedral was built over his tomb, becoming a holy site for pilgrims.

Today, the Camino is still traveled by thousands of pilgrims each year. While most people no longer walk with religious intentions, the miles convey a deep sense of community and shared life among all those walking. It is common to strike up conversations with those that you meet, to share a coffee after the early morning hours departures, or to chat throughout the evenings in the pilgrims' hostels.

Our two-month expedition consisted of waking up at 5 a.m. and walking somewhere between 15–25 miles. From our starting point in Cahors, France, Chantal and I would walk a total of 700 miles. As the path continued to lead us east, it became a time of tremendous introspection and prayer for me, the kind of thinking that can only be sustained in silence and with the simplicity of one who carries all their possessions on their back. Many of the judgments I arrived at over the course of that summer not only answered my personal questions, but also revealed a new path to follow in my teaching.

The experience of the Camino was one of grit, first in the most obvious sense, as something that begged for tenacity and determination to complete. However, it also became an experience of grit as conceived of in the research of Angela Duckworth, a psychologist and professor at the University of Pennsylvania and author of the book *Grit: the Power of Passion and Perseverance*. On her website, she defines grit as "the tendency to sustain interest and effort toward very long-term goals."[151] In the second part of her book, Duckworth describes ways in which to cultivate "grit from the inside out" including two key elements: interest and purpose.

Interest, as Duckworth draws out, is an essential part of grit. It is hard to persevere when one is apathetic about the task at hand. However, she also explains that interest is not simply created in an individual, "through introspection. Instead, interests are triggered by interactions with the outside world. The process of interest discovery can by messy, serendipitous, and inefficient. This is because you can't really predict with certainty what will capture your attention and what won't."[152] Interest in something is not invented but revealed, often as one explores.

My desire to keep on walking (rather than taking a bus or taxi) was not only about reaching Santiago, my known and stated goal. My desire was also linked to an openness to reality that was being generated in me. The miles that were most significant were not the miles that I walked the fastest or most effectively used my walking poles. The miles became precious when I was attentive and open to receive whatever came my way, when I allowed myself to be surprised and captivated by a beautiful view or the joy of an unexpected walking companion. The miles that carried the most meaning were precisely those that could not be reduced to my own effort.

---

151 Duckworth, A. (no date). Research, https://angeladuckworth.com/research/.
152 Duckworth, A. (2016). *Grit: the Power of Passion and Perseverance*. Simon and Schuster, 104.

This is a conviction that I have tried to share with my students. Teaching always implies negotiating with disinterested students who are confident that they could never be struck by studying the French Revolution or westward expansion. It requires a shift in mindset to move through the school year with the conviction that each class period offers the possibility to discover something new. The joy of discovery provides a catalyst for renewed vigor in inquiry, thinking, and reflection and introduces curiosity and wonder as essential pedagogical starting points.

The second key element in cultivating grit is purpose. Duckworth explains that "human beings have evolved to seek meaning and purpose,"[153] describing how "gritty people see their ultimate aims as deeply connected to the world beyond themselves."[154] One is motivated to work hard when they see a job or responsibility elevated to a calling in life. This importance of purpose and relevance as a driving force is a common theme in theories of motivation, such as self-determination theory[155] and expectancy value theory.[156]

My Camino was not merely a hike across Europe. Rather, my walking coincided with knowing that my intentions and questions were being taken up by the great history of many hundreds of thousands of pilgrims who had walked this same path throughout the centuries, ultimately to be entrusted to St. James in Santiago de Compostela to bring to the Lord. This sense of belonging to a community greater than myself was a valuable companion on my journey. Grit does not mean that you have all the competencies from the beginning but that you are willing to fail and grow in pursuance of a goal. To be converted. Grit is interwoven with a growth mindset and a sense of belonging and purpose.

It is for this reason that I do not shy away from introducing ultimate ends into my teaching practice. My students often complete journal activities

---

153 Ibid., 147.
154 Ibid., 148.
155 Deci, E. L. and Ryan, R. M. (2000). "The 'What' and 'Why' of Goal Pursuits: Human Needs and the Self-Determination of Behavior." *Psychological Inquiry*, 11(4), 227–68.
156 Barron, K. E. and Hulleman, C. S. (2015). "Expectancy-Value-Cost Model of Motivation." In *International Encyclopedia of the Social & Behavioral Sciences* (pp. 503–9). Elsevier.

that ask them to ponder the nature of justice and freedom by considering how these ideals have been either exalted or manipulated in different eras. Much of history can be viewed through the lens of a dialectic or a will to power, but is this what the heart longs for? Students are willing to work hard—hard enough that it begs for tenacity and determination, for grit, to complete—to seek the answer to a question that helps them to make sense of their own life and desire.

Arriving in Santiago and completing the Camino illuminated a paradox of grit. Grit is more than buckling down and trying harder. It also implies responding to what is given and allowing oneself to be changed as you move toward a greater horizon. And now, that's a journey I am taking with my students every year.

Amy Hamm teaches upper school history at St. Andrew's.

Part V

Secondary Part 3: Getting It Out: Assignments and Assessments to Make Students Think Hard

Rigor and Assessment in the 21st-Century Classroom

If you really want to see how innovative a school is, inquire about its thinking and practices regarding assessments.

What images and emotions does the word "assessment" conjure up in your mind? How many of these are negative? Stress, fear, late-night cramming, number 2 pencils and multiple-choice questions? These are all associated with the traditional ways individuals have been and continue to be assessed for knowledge and skills. Don't get me wrong, there is still a place for such traditional assessments of student learning in preparation for standardized tests such as ERBs, AP exams, SATs, and college mid-term exams. Fortunately, one of the values of an independent school education such as St. Andrew's is that it is not constrained by the drill and kill assessment strategy of other learning environments.

Assessment happens every day at St. Andrew's, and research on assessment is particularly strong. It has led St. Andrew's teachers to further expand the types of assessments students take at all grade levels and recognize that every assessment is a learning opportunity. In fact, if you were to explore St. Andrew's curriculum maps, you will see nearly 100 assessment types listed from the preschool through 12th grade. They are authentic to their academic discipline and rich in 21st-century skills.

But research has also led to a more holistic look at assessment to help provide students the opportunity to truly demonstrate what they have mastered or still need to learn. The research also reinforces some foundational thinking at St. Andrew's: families do not need to choose between an academically rigorous learning environment and a nurturing and supportive program for their children. They can have both.

At St. Andrew's, our thinking about assessment is rooted in neuromythology-busting. A neuromyth is "an imaginary or unverifiable claim about the brain."[157] Three of the most perpetuated neuromyths that directly relate to assessment center around multiple intelligences (MI) theory, learning styles, and right versus left brain thinking.

Despite a lack of verifiable scientific research at this point, the theory of multiple intelligences and learning styles, and right versus left brain thinking, has led to the belief that children should be tested according to their preferential "intelligence" or learning style. That is, a visual learner should receive and demonstrate their knowledge through visual representation or an auditory learner should receive test questions orally. This is a neuromyth. Such thinking ignores the complexity and interconnectivity of brain functions.

What research shows is that both hemispheres of the brain, left and right, are engaged in nearly all thinking activities. One of my favorite educational researchers, Paul Howard-Jones's own work concludes that, "the general processing complexity of the brain makes it unlikely that a theory resembling MI [or learning styles] will ever emerge from it."[158]

So how does this research impact assessment at St. Andrew's? Think of this as a challenge to teachers to embed richness in assessments, to think about the whole brain when designing assessments for their class or individual students. We recognize that students have areas of evolving strength and weakness, passion and disinterest. When we get the richness right, all brains are challenged and supported. What is great about the human brain is its ability to change, a process often referred to as plasticity. When teachers create rich assessments, we are agents of change.

Every year, every student will be assessed in multiple ways that are developmentally appropriate. This is what differentiated assessment

157 Tokuhama-Espinosa, T. (2010). *The New Science of Teaching and Learning.* Teachers College Press, 24.

158 Howard-Jones, P. (2010). *Introducing Neuroeducational Research: Neuroscience, Education, and the Brain from Contexts to Practice.* Routledge, 22.

means at St. Andrew's. For example, in my own history class, students are assessed via what might be considered traditional means, such as a scholarly research paper or timed, multiple-choice-test. But alternative assessments are also critical for developing multiple mind skills and enhancing student engagement. Such alternative assessments include a student-facilitated class discussion, a scored debate, video documentary project, geography quiz, active reading of primary sources, document analysis, online quiz or discussion and poster design project. Some of these assessments will play to a student's strength while others will pose significant challenges; some assessments will, wonderfully, do both.

There is another value to providing students with a range of assessment types. They call for students to learn the essential skills for success in today's world, such as critical thinking, problem solving, communication, collaboration, resiliency, and grit. These skills are best developed through alternative assessments, in particular project-based learning.

Projects enhance student engagement. We also know that when students can own their learning choices, and make an emotional connection to the material, then learning is enhanced. Moreover, when students are challenged to demonstrate their learning in a more authentic, purposeful way, such as performance-based final exams in languages or the nationally recognized American Century Oral History Project, they become more engaged and actually learn more. As Daniel Willingham points out, "A teacher's goal should always be to get students to think about meaning."[159] Alternative assessments do just that.

What does this different approach to assessment mean for the high achieving student? I would go so far as to suggest that St. Andrew's approach to assessment makes earning an A even more prestigious and valuable. As an example, one of St. Andrew's most accomplished students was taken out of his comfort zone of success on traditional tests when challenged to conduct a chemistry lab practical exam. This produced good stress for this student because it challenged him to apply knowledge and use skills in ways that more traditional assessments do not demand. It engaged this student to work harder outside of his comfort zone.

---

159 Willingham, D. (2009). *Why Don't Students Like School?* John Wiley & Sons, 61.

So what have been the most important, research-informed, changes in how teachers think about assessment for their students?

- Teachers use more formative assessments, a self-reflective process in which feedback is used by the learner for improvement, such as ungraded (thus low stress) surprise quizzes. Frequent formative assessments, both in class and online, allow students to practice recalling knowledge from their long- and short-term memory. Frequent retrieval of information significantly enhances recall ability. This is called the "testing effect."

- Teachers make returning assessments at a faster rate a priority because research shows that "when grades are expected soon the threat of disappointment is more salient.[160]" As a result, students strive to perform better on each assessment.

- Teachers provide students a range of assessments. A noticeable difference is the opportunities for students to visually demonstrate knowledge whether through two- and three-dimensional art work or other forms of digital and social media.

- Teachers provide student test correction opportunities. Delaying or scaffolding feedback, and having students struggle with finding the correct answer, leads to better retention than does simply providing correct answers.

- Teachers recognize that periodically providing a student a chance to choose an assessment type enhances the student's investment and motivation in their learning. For example, students taking United States/European history to 1860 year-end final exam can choose between a more traditional, two-hour final exam, or the more visual Historical Head project. As one student said, "it's not easier, it's just hard in a different way."

- Teachers ask students to reflect on what neurodevelopmental demands—attention, memory, spatial or temporal sequential ordering, language, neuromotor function, social or higher-order cognition—a particular assessment might be placing on their brains to decide the appropriate study strategies. This includes

160 Rinne, L. (2012). "Neuroeducation: How Evidence from Psychology, Cognitive Science, and Neuroscience Can Improve Teaching and Learning." Presentation given at St. Andrew's Episcopal School, 12 January.

providing students an opportunity to reflect on their assessment performance, how well their study strategies worked, and how they might study differently next time.

- Teachers differentiate for their students between active studying versus passive, "traditional" studying, and why the former enhances long-term memory retention. Teachers also help students find active studying strategies that work for them. Remember, we are building skills for their future—what skills can we equip a student with that will enhance their ability to be successful with the memory demands of law school or medical school?

As the designers of each of their classes, it is the teachers who decide the appropriate assessment for a certain body of knowledge or skill. That is why it is so critical that at St. Andrew's, the entire faculty and academic leadership has training in how the mind learns and how research informs decisions around assessment. Such research means that the ways in which a student's knowledge, skills, and understanding are measured today are a lot broader than the majority of those who are reading this article experienced in their own academic journey.

And that is a good thing.

Glenn Whitman is the Dreyfuss Family Director of the Center for Transformative Teaching and Learning at St. Andrew's (www.thecttl. org) and is co-author of *Neuroteach: Brain Science and the Future of Education.*

Brain Changer

As an Episcopal school, service to others is encoded in St. Andrew's DNA. It is part and parcel of who we are, included in our mission statement, and incorporated into curriculum and community life alike.

In keeping with the teachings of most major religious traditions, we understand ourselves to be called by God to love our neighbors—which is to say, the neighbors we know and the neighbors we have yet to meet. This means genuinely caring for and about other people, providing for their needs as appropriate, and offering a compassionate, empathetic ear whenever possible. While a life shaped by service is rarely "easy" or "comfortable," the benefits of service can be life-changing.

In addition to contributing to our Episcopal identity, service is essential to St. Andrew's mission because it leads to growth. We all know this intuitively. At its core, service invites us to redirect our gaze—even if only briefly—away from our own interests and desires. This, in turn, cannot help but expand our worldview. We understand this at St. Andrew's, which is why, from our youngest children raising money to buy goats for our sister school in Haiti, to our 12th graders devoting 60 hours to in-depth community service before graduation, every student has multiple opportunities over the course of his or her school career to grow through serving others.

What is particularly exciting for us as educators is to hear students articulate their experiences with service—including both the joys and the challenges. Upon returning from a service trip in downtown Washington, an eighth grader offered the following reflection in Chapel:

Unlike the other service sites I had worked at previously, I was interacting face-to-face with the needy community of the D.C. area. Originally I had wanted to work in the kitchen. I had purposely intended not to interact with these people. Luckily for me, though I didn't know it at the time, the opportunity passed for me to participate in the food preparation. Instead I got to experience something that many people never get to do. I got to meet and talk directly with people in need.

This student's shift, from concern over contact with "these people" to embracing with enthusiasm the opportunity to meet and talk with folks in need, points to a fairly dramatic sea-change in relatively short order. These connections are transformative. As they start to imagine themselves in the shoes of the other, students flex their empathy and compassion muscles in new—and perhaps altogether surprising—ways.

But what does all of this have to do with neuroscience? How does serving others shape not only students' character but also their malleable brains?

It turns out that the effects of service on brain development are myriad. Renowned psychologist Daniel Goleman, who is perhaps best known for his work with "emotional intelligence," has collaborated in recent years with the Dalai Lama, himself a dedicated student of neuroscience. By studying the brain scans of Buddhist monks during meditations designed to promote feelings of compassion, Goleman discovered what he refers to as a "brain shift" when compassion is generated. Goleman concludes that, "The very act of concern for others' well-being... creates a greater state of well-being within oneself."[161]

Clearly Goleman's findings have important implications for schools, where students regularly do battle with feelings of stress and fear. When the amygdala, the emotional center in the brain, is assaulted by fear or stress, both short-term memory retention and higher-order cognition are impacted negatively.[162] But studies show that the converse is also true: when the anterior cingulate, the structure in the brain associated with empathy, is active, "attention, working memory, motivation, and many

161 Goleman, D. (2003). *Destructive Emotions: How Can We Overcome Them: A Conversation with the Dalai Lama.* Bantam.
162 LeDoux, J. (1996). *The Emotional Brain.* Simon & Schuster.

other executive functions" are improved.[163] This underscores the value of placing students in situations in which they have an opportunity to experience feelings of empathy and compassion for others. By developing caring relationships through service, students reap significant neuro-educational benefits that impact their own learning.

In addition to shaping students' ability to empathize with others, service learning also has been shown to stimulate the brain simply by virtue of its nature and design. We know that exposure to novel conditions and stimuli—such as the student who couldn't hide in the kitchen—helps the brain to grow in new ways.[164] As well, service learning provides a context in which students can make connections between content learned in the classroom and its application in "real-life."

So how do we, as parents and educators, leverage these many brain-beneficial effects of service learning for our own students? To begin, we can support our young people's enthusiasm for service by providing opportunities to participate in up-close-and-personal, face-to-face experiences that will enable them to build up their compassion muscles. In addition, and perhaps even more importantly, we must give students a chance to reflect on their experiences in order to mine them for what they've learned. Research literature bears out the importance of reflection as "the transformative link between the action of serving and the ideas and understanding of learning."[165]

At St. Andrew's, faculty offer such metacognitive moments in which students are asked to think about what and how they learn, all the time. Whether it is through journal exercises or class discussions, informal bus ride conversations or Chapel talks, students are challenged regularly to interpret and extract meaning from their service of others. This provides an opportunity to acknowledge any preconceived stereotypes or reservations they might have harbored, as well as to claim their own struggles to make peace with a world still marked by social and economic disparity.

163 Newberg, M. D. and Waldman, M. R. (2009). *How God Changes Your Brain: Breakthrough Findings from a Leading Neuroscientist.* Random House.

164 Gregory, G. and Chapman, C. (2002). *Differentiated Instructional Strategies: One Size Doesn't Fit All.* Corwin Press.

165 Kinloch, B. and Liptrot, J. L. (2010). *Making the Journey Meaningful: Why Our Brains LOVE Service Learning!* Texas Summer Institute.

St. Andrew's students are groomed for service from a very young age, and they love it. The fact that it also helps to improve their sense of well-being, their social cognition, their higher-order cognition, and their problem-solving skills is icing on the cake.[166] Perhaps we need not let them know how "good it is for them," lest it somehow diminish the appeal. The brain-based benefits of service can remain our little secret!

WHAT SERVICE LOOKS LIKE IN THE NINTH GRADE CLASSROOM

For the past seven years, St. Andrew's ninth-grade service learning students have discovered firsthand the issues of homelessness. By having a meal and a conversation at Loaves and Fishes with local homeless men, women, and children; by selling newspapers for their assigned vendor from Street Sense; by chopping carrots at DC Central Kitchen; by boxing canned goods for Capital Area Food Bank; and by gleaning food for local shelters.

One student in the service learning class remarked, "I wasn't sure what to expect from our first service learning trip, but I knew I needed to be open-minded and step out of my comfort zone. Going into the Samaritan Ministry's office helped me see how helpful and effective they can really be. I also benefited from hearing the real, true-life stories of some of the participants. It's amazing to me to see how much Samaritan Ministry can do for the homeless."

Another student said "the first thing I think of when I see a homeless person is odd. I don't want to talk to them. When we went to Loaves and Fishes, I talked to a man who was homeless, but he acted like a normal person, just like me."

In Mary Helen Immordino-Yang and Antonio Damasio's article, "We Feel, Therefore We Learn: The Relevance of Affective and Social Neuroscience to Education," the authors state, "As recent advances in the neurobiology of emotions reveal, in the real world, cognition functions in the service of life-regulating goals, implemented by emotional machinery. As educators have long known, it is simply not enough for students to master knowledge and logical reasoning skills in the traditional academic sense. They must

---

166 Eyler, J., Giles, D. E. and Schmiede, A. (1996). *A Practitioner's Guide to Reflection in Service-Learning: Student Voices and Reflections.* Vanderbilt University.

be able to choose among and recruit these skills and knowledge usefully outside of the structured context of a school or laboratory."[167]

At St. Andrew's, we believe that our service learning program provides our students with the crucial opportunities to go outside of the structured environment of the classroom and learn about themselves and others in meaningful and powerful ways.

Patricia Alexander was chaplain to the middle and upper schools and head of the philosophy and religion department during the writing of this research-informed article.

Ginger Cobb is Head of the Upper School and Co-Director of Service Learning.

---

167 Immordino-Yang, M. H. and A. Damasio, A. (2007). "We Feel, Therefore We Learn: The Relevance of Affective and Social Neuroscience to Education." *Mind, Brain, and Education,* (1)1, 3-10. See also: Elaine B. Johnson, Service Learning Stimulates the Brain (The World and I Online) 146+.

Variations on a Theme

> *All the books are questions for me. I write them because I don't know something.*
> **—Toni Morrison**

For Toni Morrison, the writing process is essentially exploratory—a question, not an answer. This is a crucial attitude for beginning any academic pursuit. Authentic education begins when we simply "don't know something" and decide that we want to learn. So we find an interesting plot of land, grab the best shovel we know how to wield, and start digging around in the dirt.

Unfortunately, for too many students, education is more about answers than questions. Novels, for instance, are really about "themes," otherwise known as "those annoying, hidden things that English teachers can see and that Sparknotes and Shmoop will list for me." Like many educational concepts, the word "theme" should be a helpful digging tool, but for some students themes are prepackaged crossword-puzzle answers such as "The Duality of Man" or "Appearance vs. Reality." Such terms are vague and cliche, but they can still be fruitful points of embarkation (What is the appearance? What is it covering? Why?). The problem is that many students stop thinking and questioning at precisely the point they should begin, deciding they have found the "right" answer.

In his essay, "The Loss of the Creature," American novelist Walker Percy described this tendency of students to stop thinking for themselves in terms of a failure to look past "educational packaging." Percy wrote, "A student who has the desire to get at a dogfish or a Shakespearean sonnet may have the greatest difficulty in salvaging the creature itself from the educational package in which it is presented." Any teacher knows that a certain amount of "packaging" is essential. Especially when it comes to tasks that require higher-order cognition and creativity, students need protocols to follow and models to copy. You can't just throw students in a room with books, chemistry sets, and math problems, hoping for the best. However, when students get too comfortable with a particular package, there is a danger that they have mastered a school task (such as "write a decent essay") without getting much better at more fundamental things (such as "figure out how to say what I really think about something complicated").

I think most teachers understand this instinctively; we try to keep things fresh and to give students options to shake them out of these ruts whenever we can. Educational research calls this using "novelty" and "choice," and these strategies have been proven to be effective.

Studies have convincingly shown us that adding novelty and choice to a curriculum increases student engagement and leads to deeper thinking.[168, 169] This research also confirms my belief that all students are capable of intellectual curiosity and academic passion; we just have to help unlock them. My favorite moments as a teacher have occurred when a student gets authentically interested in an assignment and moves from "can I just say enough smart-sounding things in this essay?" to "What is Morrison really up to in this novel? How can I say something new and interesting?" When this happens, you can almost see the lights turn on.

But how do we help turn those lights on more consistently? One way that I have increasingly included in my teaching involves "repackaging" not just classroom activities and lessons, but major assessments as well. I have tried to incorporate novelty, choice, and playfulness into my teaching for a long time, and these strategies are often successful in terms of increasing student engagement and critical thinking. However, until a few years ago, I was skeptical of radically changing up the educational package of

168 Katz, I. and Assor, A. (2007). "When Choice Motivates and When It Does Not." *Educational Psychology Review*, 19(4) 429–42.

169 Ryan, R. M. and Deci, E. L. (2000). "Self-Determination Theory and the Facilitation of Intrinsic Motivation, Social Development, and Well-Being." *American Psychologist*, 55(1), 68.

the traditional literary analysis. I think I was afraid that doing so would somehow not be difficult or serious enough for students, but I have come to see that play can be very serious business.

What is real intellectual work if not playing with different interpretations of the world? If there is no buy in and no sense of play to what a student is doing, they will be merely mimicking learned motions to a large degree. My thinking began to shift two years ago when I started teaching English 10: Great Works with my colleagues Susheela Robinson and Andrew Seidman. While the course still includes traditional essays, it also features several novel and engaging major assessments that still assess a range of "traditional" skills, such as literary analysis and rhetorical prowess. These assessments shift the educational package more radically, giving weaker students a fresh start and throwing stronger students off their well-worn rails in a fruitful way. The result is often a more powerful and authentic learning experience.

One of my favorite examples of such an assessment is the "podcast project" we created to replace the final exam. This project is highly flexible and can be tinkered with from year to year, but the basic structure is simple: students create a professional-sounding podcast that explores a topic of their choice from different angles. In other words, the podcasts are repackaged "theme" essays. The goal is still to dive deeply into a specific idea, but the new wrapping paper makes all the difference. We have found that the students write more organically and naturally about their topics than on traditional essays. The writing feels more like an authentic exploration of topics like race, love, identity, and family and less like "something I have to do for school."

One reason the podcast project is so successful is the simple novelty of creating an audio recording as opposed to a written text. We ask students to create three different "segments" to their podcast, and the most traditional of these segments is a standard literary analysis tracing their chosen topic in two works we read together. All of the students have written theme analyses before, but none of them have had to record their work as a podcast.

The change in format helps students avoid merely going through the motions, and the fact that they know they will play the podcast for their peers also helps them consider audience: an important skill for any writer. They not only catch more editing errors, they are also better at noticing confusing, shallow, or redundant ideas. For many students, they simply seem to work harder to make their ideas interesting and clear. It may be that some students have decided "I'm just not good at essays," whereas a podcast, even a literary one, feels like a fresh start.

The other two segments of the podcast change from year to year, but we always aim to help students find aspects of their topic that they are authentically interested in and that are connected to their own lives. For example, last year we created a segment in which students crafted persuasive arguments about a current social issue related to their topic. Because all of the topics are also important to the literature we have already read together, these segments help form a crucial bridge between the classroom and the larger world.

We also usually include a "free choice" segment in which students can discuss their topic from any angle and in any format they want. This is the segment of the podcast that students love the most, and it has also led to outstanding results, again showing that deep, creative thinking often follows once kids are "hooked" and given choices. Students have produced CNN-style roundtable debates, This American Life-style narratives, love-advice hotlines, and hilarious but thoughtful fake celebrity interviews.

For this level of freedom to work, it is important to set students up for success with clear but highly flexible rubrics and many, many models. We also have students create a number of "just for fun" podcasts leading up to the real one to decrease anxiety and encourage a healthy sense of playfulness. Too much freedom, like too much "packaging" and guidance, can lead to fear and anxiety that stifles authentic, creative thinking. Before deciding how to tackle their free choice segment, students listen to a wide array of real podcasts, thinking about which models they want to imitate and about how to put their own spin on things.

This parallels real-world thinking and problem solving. It is important to learn from previous models, templates, and "packages," but we also need to think critically and creatively about how they could be different. This is true of almost any task that a human can do better than a computer: from writing a speech, to designing a shoe, to making a podcast. For these tasks, there are guidelines and instructions to be found, but at some point, we need to make our own judgements and, like Morrison, learn to ask our own questions. "Is it good enough? How can I make it better? How can I put my own, new spin on it?" These can be terrifyingly open-ended questions even for adults.

I believe that helping our kids become more comfortable thinking this way and helping them learn to enjoy the "digging" as much as arriving at the right answer will set them up for success both in a college classroom and beyond.

Morgan Evans teaches upper school English at St. Andrew's where he is also head of the English department and a wrestling coach.

Metacognition in Action Across Disciplines

Picture this: two colleagues divided by discipline but connected by research; detached by division but united by mission. As members of both the CTTL team and St. Andrew's faculty, we are often immersed in conversations about research, which we apply in our own math and English classes.

One subject fascinated both of us because of its difficulty to explain in our CTTL work: metacognition. In its simplest form, metacognition means thinking about one's thinking. Additionally, metacognition can be thought of as using past experiences to navigate a better path through one's current work.[170]

Honing metacognitive skills empowers students with self-knowledge that they can apply beyond classroom walls. But how can teachers help students gain this important but underappreciated set of skills? What does metacognition in action look like?

Students often enter both math and English classes with a fixed mindset. We often hear students saying things like: "I'm not a math person" or "I'm not a good writer." But having students practice identifying their thought processes and which steps they took to solve a problem or write an essay helps them shift their mindset. Our goal is to empower students with the ability to use their past as a tool rather than feel defeated by it.

---

170 Education Endowment Foundation. (no date). Metacognition and Self-Regulation, https://educationendowmentfoundation.org.uk/evidence-summaries/teaching-learning-toolkit/meta-cognition-and-self-regulation.

BUILD A CULTURE OF QUESTIONING

"You shouldn't take Tylenol before you have a headache." This line, often said by a fellow SAES math teacher, has changed how I plan my classes. As a student, I felt I was taught a skill like solving proportions and then given time to practice the skill, never fully understanding what a proportion was or why I was solving it in this way. This focus on surface-level algorithms rather than deep understanding stops students' desire to think and grow since the thinking has already been done for them. They leave knowing how to solve that problem but not understanding or appreciating the concepts that would allow them to solve marginally related problems.

My approach now is to help them use prior knowledge in a new context by beginning class with an open-ended question. I choose questions that are somewhat related to what they already know but that particularly at first glance, feel totally new. This allows students the time needed to access their "toolbox" and think metacognitively about which problem-solving strategies to employ rather than being given the tool they will need to solve each problem.

These problems can be incredibly frustrating but eventually rewarding for students. To support them in this endeavor, students are required to ask questions, which eliminates the, "Ms. Magner, I don't get this!" Encouraging students to ask questions forces them to think about their own thinking. The best part about this rule is that most of the time simply creating the question is enough to get them started on the problem themselves!

I used to think students needed to be explicitly taught how to apply their existing skills and knowledge into a new context. But now I know that students benefit more from being active participants when learning how to apply existing knowledge into a new context, and that it is my job to pick a new context that is not too hard and not too easy so they have productive struggle.[171]

---

171 This "I used to think but now I think (know)" is adapted from the Visible Thinking Routines designed by Ron Ritchhart as part of Project Zero at Harvard University's Graduate School of Education.

MODEL IT OURSELVES: THINK ALOUD

In English, often I assign reading/annotating for homework. But I have realized that reading during class is an opportunity to model metacognition. Reading aloud in class, pausing periodically to ask students questions about the plot and literary terms, is a way to model active reading. I encourage my students to ask their own questions as we read, emphasizing the importance of actively, critically engaging with the text—using their previous experiences to help them navigate through their current thinking, which is at the heart of metacognition. I have noticed that when I model for my students in this way, they are more engaged and eager to add their own opinions, questions, and theories as to what will happen next. During these read alouds, students can more clearly appreciate the complexity of the thinking process during active reading.

I used to think that students should intuitively know how to annotate. But now I know that modeling helps students understand what it means to actively read.

In math class, my students love volunteering to solve problems on the whiteboard, but I noticed that students have a hard time explaining their thinking, which indicates they are having a hard time thinking about their own thinking. During the first few weeks of school, I model my own problem-solving process a lot. I explain each step of solving a multi-step equation, sharing why I chose to subtract 2 before I divided each side by 3, for example. I also mention the numerous ways I could have approached a problem and justify to the class why I ultimately chose one way over the other. When students go to the board to do a problem, the expectation is that they also talk out each step and why they chose it. I continue to verbalize my own problem-solving process throughout the year to help build a classroom culture where thinking about our own thinking is the norm.

I used to think that students needed more time to practice problems on their own, but now I know that while this is still true, it is helped by my modeling the problem-solving process to the whole class.

MOVE BEYOND REFLECTION:

Precision Is Key

Both teachers and students confuse metacognition and reflection; metacognition stems from reflection, but not all reflection leads to metacognition. In his book *How We Think*, educational philosopher John Dewey thinks of metacognition as a type of reflection about one's own way of thinking.[172] As teachers, we ask students to reflect on many things, but if we want students to work actively on building their metacognitive skills, we need to take them on a reflective journey that leads them to analyze their own thinking processes. This goes significantly beyond asking them how well they think they did on a test.

In English class, I explicitly taught my students three strategies for memorizing vocabulary: self-testing, revisiting the words in context, and visualizing their vocabulary. I then handed back to the students their last vocabulary quiz and asked them to write about how they prepared for the quiz, how that study method worked or didn't work, and which of the three new strategies they would employ for the next quiz.

I later had an honest conversation with one of my students who, after failing the quiz, asked me for additional help. He admitted that he had studied by himself during the early morning hours the day of the quiz. We discussed how he could leverage his verbal expressive skills to learn vocabulary through conversation, one of his favorite pastimes. Through this process, together we walked the metacognitive walk, thinking about how he approached the problem before, what didn't work, and what usually does work when he's processing ideas: talking.

I used to think post assessment free form reflection was enough to improve learning. But now I know that structured opportunities for students to think about their own thinking are more effective.

In math class, there is this phenomena of "silly mistakes." What I have learned in my time teaching middle school math is that anything can be labeled a silly mistake, including: adding two numbers incorrectly, not distributing the negative, not following order of operations; the list

---

172 Dewey, J. (2008). *How We Think*. Cosimo.

goes on and on. I avoid using over-simplistic labels like "silly mistake." Instead, I emphasize the power of mistakes because of how much we can learn from them.

After each assessment, students do an error analysis of any mistakes they made. I noticed that unless students fully understand the mistakes they made, they won't learn anything from them. Calling mistakes "silly" or "careless" takes the ownership away from the students. Instead of using these terms, I provide students with more precise observations of their mistakes to ensure they fully understand what went wrong so that they do not make the same mistake again. Students then have to reflect back on their thinking and their problem-solving process to see where they went wrong. For example, adding 7 + 2 and getting 8 isn't simply a "silly" mistake to make; instead, it is a computation error and means that students need to check their work as they solve problems.

I used to think having students do quiz corrections was enough. But now I know that precision of language is necessary for students to truly learn from their mistakes.

Practice What You Preach

Students shouldn't be the only ones practicing metacognition. Ask yourself the following questions to expand your own metacognitive skills: Why did I structure my lesson in that particular way? What would I like to learn how to do better? What am I confused about?

One simple way to put this into practice: immediately after class, write in your lesson plan a short note about what went well, what didn't go well, and what you'd like to do next time as a guide for your next lesson.

In addition, you may have noticed that after each section we added a "I used to think... but now I think" statement. This is a simple way to capture how your thinking has changed: try using it yourself and with your students!

We used to think that math and English teachers couldn't learn from each other.

But now we know metacognition is applicable across disciplines!

Molly Magner taught middle school math and was the CTTL's Digital Content Manager, and Julia Dean taught upper school English and was the CTTL's Program Development and Innovation Associate during the writing of this research-informed article.

Taking a Plunge into the Depths of Choice

Biology has been a subject that traditionally requires extensive memorization. It still does, in our opinion—it makes more sense to talk about how a cell functions if you can remember what the different parts do, without having to look up "endoplasmic reticulum" or "mitochondria" every time you see those words. Having key knowledge stored in your long-term memory frees up space in your active working memory for learning new material.

So each year our final exam in biology tends to require a great deal of memorization—different phyla in the animal kingdom, facts about evolution and plants, the basics of cell biology, and protein synthesis. You may remember some of these terms from your own school days. While there are several questions that also ask students to analyze data, make predictions, and engage in other critical-thinking tasks, the final exam does tend to play to the strengths of those kids who memorize more easily than others.

And that became an obstacle as we worked to make our biology course as research-informed and brain-friendly as possible. Think about how much stress a high-stakes end-of-year test, which you get one shot at doing well on, can induce. We know that some stress can be productive for a student. But high levels of stress tend to engage "fight-or-flight" areas of the brain, shunting incoming information such as a question on an exam (e.g. "Explain the role of the stigma in flower reproduction.") to the reactionary part of your brain, rather than engaging the prefrontal cortex, where thoughtful analysis and synthesis of an answer takes place. This is not brain-friendly for many students. Some do thrive on the intellectual challenge, to be sure! But why subject all students to this when there's more than one authentic way to assess learning?

Choice, in and of itself, is a wonderful tool that we can use to differentiate for students while still giving them authentic challenge. This final assessment is a challenge, but we can use the fact that our students have strengths in a variety of areas to their advantage. So, while we definitely want and expect each student to learn and appreciate the various topics and concepts in biology, how about permitting their knowledge to be assessed in a variety of ways?

We are not advocating that we make a separate final exam for each student, based on perceived strengths and weaknesses. That is not brain-friendly, either, as it doesn't allow students to push themselves into rigorous scenarios that ultimately satisfy and reward them. Meeting a challenge is a major part of learning as well; it is important for students to experience these moments when they are unsure of the path to success and have to figure out a strategy that works for them. We instead are arguing that for the final assessment, different kids can meet different challenges.

So, this past year we held our breath and took the plunge into the depths of choice for our biology classes. We offered the choice of a traditional final exam or the creation of a "Bill Nye the Science Guy" type video that took a deep dive into a particular topic. We initially worried that these assessments would be challenging to compare, as a comprehensive 12-page paper-and-pencil test doesn't seem to require the same mastery of a single topic, such as the process of transpiration. However, we felt that ending a course of study with substantial knowledge was the ultimate goal. It might be a broad overarching knowledge of factual content, or it might be taking one concept and wrestling with how to make it understandable (and watchable) by a viewer. To truly teach a concept, one must have a deep understanding of the concept and related material, so as to put it in the proper context. And, at a fundamental level, isn't that what learning is all about?

So, with all that in mind, we allowed our biology students to have a choice in their final assessment this year. We provided review sheets with practice material for the students who opted for the traditional paper-and-pencil test, and we created guidelines and a grading rubric for the students who were making a video.

At first it was very stressful for some students, who didn't know which option to choose. They were not sure how to assess this type of choice, so we heard questions like:

"Can we take both and see which one we do better on?" (The answer here was "No!")

"Which one do you think I should do?"

"Which one do you think is easier?"

They had so many questions! And we teachers didn't have answers to most of their questions.

We told them to think about it, consider the options, and perhaps discuss them with their parents. Students then filled out a Google form to make their choice: traditional assessment or instructional video. If they chose to create a video, we asked them to indicate whether they would work alone or with partners. We stressed to them that they needed to choose partners wisely to be sure they succeeded.

Approximately 40% of students choose the traditional paper-and-pencil exam. They were armed with the tools to take that type of test and knew they could study and pull themselves together to perform well. The other 60% was willing to try something very new. They had a topic and a rubric that helped them know how to be successful. They were bravely venturing into the unknown to create a final exam. Were they Bill Nye fans, maybe? We are. Did they crave the creativity? Did they just want to avoid one traditional exam? We will never really know, but that's OK.

After a day, three groups of students opted to switch from traditional exam to video exam. Some students asked to work alone, and we decided to permit this since the assessment wasn't necessarily about collaboration (though for groups, that was a necessary component for being successful).

Students were required to use a shared Google doc to submit a list of required words, a script of the video, and references so that we had a checkpoint on their progress. This allowed us to intervene and have documentation as to how the workflow was going. The shared document contained the project rubric and a calendar of the days in class that were available to use for video production.

The results: the students who took the traditional exam did well, most of them scoring in the range they usually did for that type of assessment. A couple of students did not do as well as they usually did; perhaps they were overwhelmed by the process or the fact that our exam took place on the final day of exam week. It gave us a chance to review the exam with that student and parent and discuss options and preparation for the following year.

The videos were fantastic. We viewed them in class on post exam reflection days. The students had thrown themselves into making clever, catchy, and creative videos to explain and teach their topic. They had created a note-taking sheet for their peers to use while watching their videos, and they took the stage as teachers. It was wonderful to see the wide variety of styles and approaches they had to solving this puzzle. The class voted on Oscar-worthy videos and performers, and we all enjoyed the experience. Several of the students who had taken the traditional exam said they wished they could restart and switch over to the alternative assessment.

Would we do it again? In a minute. It allowed for creativity at a time of year that students usually experience never-ending stress. The gift of choice allowed students to enter the last weeks of school with confidence. It put the learning in their hands. Many of the students who chose the video are students who often struggle with all types of assessment, but they did well with the defined rubric that they could follow. Plus, this project really mattered to them; they showed their funny, creative side and played with the content.

One of our favorite memories of the alternative exams was watching two ninth-grade boys host a "talk show" to teach the audience about the difference between endo and exoskeletons. They created lively, clever dialogue that showed off their theatrical sides.

In another memorable video, two girls threw themselves completely into the project and had skits, props, and demos; they even recruited a dad to ask questions they could answer within the video.

We are so proud of all our students, whether they wanted to show their knowledge with the traditional exam or the alternative video assessment. We can't wait to see next year's final exams!

Kim O'Shaughnessy teaches science while leading the FIRST Robotics Teams at St. Andrew's.

Phyllis Robinson taught biology at St. Andrew's and was a CTTL/ Omidyar Teacher Research Fellow and Neuroteach Global Mission grader.

What Great Homework Looks Like

How would you recognize a school that assigns great homework? Would you choose the one that kept students busy for the most hours at night? That seems ridiculous, doesn't it? And yet families and schools in the Washington, D.C., area seem to falsely equate hours of homework with academic rigor.

What we should all be focusing on instead is this question: What is great homework?

First, let's address the question of whether we should have homework at all.

As a professional learning community, the St. Andrew's faculty read *The End of Homework* by Etta Kralovec and John Buell a few years ago. The research on the instructional value of homework is still unfolding. There is reasonable agreement that in elementary grades reading is the best assignment. Older students appear to gain some benefit for the first hour or two and then additional time yields little result. But we also know, from our research into how minds learn best, that the type of work teachers assign really matters, too.

At St. Andrew's the students have homework. Several teachers have conducted action research of their own to discover if students benefit. By teaching without assigning homework and then teaching while assigning a reasonable amount of reflective or reinforcing questions, we noted a positive correlation with homework. But we need to get the type of homework right. Do so and we give our students the means and motivation to focus on their academics beyond the school day.

Give great homework and we get engagement that extends learning; do homework wrong and disengagement reigns supreme and performance spirals downward. Engagement is key to effective learning; with true engagement anything is possible.

Do you remember ever getting that assignment that so engrossed you that you suddenly noticed it was late at night and you had no idea how all those hours flew by? What inspired you? Did you ever get a packet of fill-in-the-blank worksheets that made your heart sink? Meaning, relevancy, or novelty lead to assignments that, even if they don't inspire that night-owl fervor, create engagement and thus learning. For example, an upper school philosophy teacher uses a short paragraph by Nietzsche with a brief paragraph response that starts with the students feeling comfortable, but that ultimately shocks them—this is the hook; a 15-minute assignment that takes the class to a higher level of discussion and thought. But this is just part of the story at St. Andrew's. We can dig deeper; what is great homework?

It begins with understanding how student minds learn best—a little research in this area makes you realize that teachers can both reduce the time students spend on homework AND increase student learning.

Some strategies are teacher driven. For example, research shows that tasks that involve synopsis and recall—like a five-minute summary essay of the day's class—help students consolidate material in their memory. The same is true of metacognitive tasks that demand students to reflect on how they are learning. Students also work to refine assignments that they have received carefully structured teacher feedback on—just enough to help them step forward, not too much to give the game away.[173] Getting this scaffolding right creates real engagement with the ideas and, research shows, helps student performance.

Another example involves chunking. The latest brain research tells us that most teenagers can hold, and this may surprise you, just three things in their active working memory at once. People get around this by chunking—we group bits of information into larger chunks so the brain thinks they are processing just one thing.

173 Finn, B. and Metcalfe, J. (2010). "Scaffolding Feedback to Maximize Long-Term Error Correction." *Memory and Cognition,* 38, 951–61.

Creating great homework includes crafting assignments that deliberately create the chunking you want. This includes memorizing factual knowledge because it frees up limited space in a student's active working memory for higher-order thinking. This is an effective, time-efficient way of increasing student performance, using time outside of class, to increase what a student can do in class.

The goal with all these assignments is quality of work, not quantity of time spent. Students recognize when they are being given quality tasks for homework—they are good at distinguishing real work from busy work and when they are being given tasks that have meaning for them. The kind of tasks that move their learning forward.

One type of homework that has been receiving increased attention is the flipped classroom that has been inspired by resources such as Khan Academy and LearnZillon.[174] One upper school math teacher who has been experimenting with "flipping" the traditional classroom model said, "I record my daily lesson and post it to the internet for the students to watch at home. In class, the students spend time working problems. The benefits are two-fold; the students can watch the video multiple times to ensure they have understood it and in class, they can ask me questions and get the necessary support while practicing with the concepts and skills."

Other strategies are institutional. For example, the St. Andrew's schedule is designed so that two days a week students take half their classes for twice as long. This is good for many reasons—a huge one being that it reduces the amount of task-switching students have to do. Students feel they do better work on the assignments they have, and this positive feedback also helps as it fosters engagement and confidence. St. Andrew's also makes sure that the conversation of what is great homework is an ongoing research topic that teachers are driving forward through the sharing of best practices based on brain research. One outcome of such research is that students who are not enrolled in Advanced Placement classes will not have homework over extended school breaks.

One important strategy is training students how to do homework. For example, research tells us that task switching (going from the 10th

---

174 Khan Academy (http://www.khanacademy.org/) and LearnZillion (http://learnzillion.com/).

math problem to Facebook or Twitter then returning to the homework) inhibits memory consolidation. Research also suggests that music at the right beat with no words, might help some tasks, but not things related to memory storage. We often coach our students to avoid listening to music when studying so that their whole brain can be engaged in what they are trying to have "stick" in their memory. Getting students to resist these behaviors is not an easy task, it goes against habit for many. To help with this, we make sure it is part of a much larger ongoing discussion with students about metacognition and self reflection. Middle and upper school students read articles such as, "What You Should Know About Your Brain." Why do this? Because as the article's author, Dr. Judy Willis states, "Teaching students the mechanism behind how the brain operates, and teaching them approaches they can use to work that mechanism more effectively, helps students believe they can create a more intelligent, creative, and powerful brain."[175] Students should know, and be honest about, what works for them as the individual learner they are. Metacognition, self-reflection, and exploring strategies are deeply ingrained parts of the St. Andrew's student experience. It is how we do school.

The best thing is that this works for all students. Everyone, no matter how strong a student, benefits from the St. Andrew's faculty's attention to great homework. Better assignments lead to better learning. A stronger set of study skills enhance student performance and potentially allow them to sleep more. And we know from research that sleep is critical to learning as it aids in memory consolidation as well as playing a critical role in immune function, metabolism, and attitude.[176]

Think of Sisyphus—the figure from Greek mythology condemned to roll the boulder to the top of a hill only to see it roll back down—as a metaphor for more traditional approaches to homework. And as he climbs, he calls out, "academic rigor equates with the size of the homework pile." So, at

---

175 Willis, J. (2009/2010). "How to Teach Students About the Brain," *Educational Leadership* 67 (December 2009/January 2010). See also: "What You Should Know About Your Brain," *Educational Leadership* (ASCD) (2007) and www.radteach.com.

176 TEDx Talks (17 July 2010). "TEDxRiverCity – Robert Stickgold – Sleep, Memory, and Dreams: Fitting the Pieces Together [YouTube], http://www.youtube.com/watch?v=WmRGNunPj3c.

St. Andrew's we proudly say, yes, our homework is indeed easier—if by "easier" you mean that it reduces the Sisyphus mindset, where students feel doomed to spend eternity pushing a boulder of disinterest up a mountain of worksheets and busy work. And it does so precisely because it is anything but trivial. It is purposeful; it is thoughtful; it is based on how we know minds learn. But it goes beyond this we are also training habits of mind, habits that our students will take with them to whatever college they attend or profession they choose. This is the heart of St. Andrew's desire to assign great homework: a mindfulness toward work that advances learning.

David Brown is Associate Head of School and Dr. Ian Kelleher teaches science at St. Andrew's and is the Dreyfuss Family Chair of Research for the Center of Transformative Teaching and Learning. He is also co-author of the book *Neuroteach: Brain Science and the Future of Education.*

From Grant to Great Works

Alexander was called it. That winding wall in China is known for it. Tony, the Tiger yelled it on every box of those sugar-crusted flakes. But what exactly did Tony mean when he declared, "They're gr-r-reat!"? What do we mean when we tell our students, athletes, fellow colleagues, or administrators that something or someone is great? Perhaps its vagueness saves us from the roll-up-your-sleeves consideration our discussions need. Perhaps the linguistic ambiguity of the word simply saves us a lot of time. But if we don't know exactly what we mean when we call a book or a poem great, then how will our students?

These questions impelled us to apply to the Center for Transformative Teaching and Learning for a Research-Informed Teaching Grant. We sought to make our 10th-grade English classrooms more student-centered and more relevant. After years of the inflexible structure of a traditional British literature course, we witnessed students falling out of love with the very subject we hoped might inspire them, so we began to research the role of choice and independence in learning. Of course, this research led to more questions, such as, what happens when students are allowed to develop a passion or select a book or investigate a concept of their choice? How does fostering a coaching relationship with students, where they can develop their own voices with guidance from a teacher who knows them, impact lasting learning and intellectual curiosity?

In his 2013 book *The Social Neuroscience of Education: Optimizing Attachment and Learning in the Classroom*, Louis Cozolino says, "We can increase classroom autonomy by offering choices, encouraging independent problem solving, and involving students in decision making.

All of these actions promote intrinsic motivation, self-determination, and the students' ability to discern the causes of their successes and failures." St. Andrew's strives to foster an environment where students develop their intrinsic motivation and self-determination. From this, the Great Works project was born. In the Great Works project, we explored, along with our students, how teaching and learning changed when students could make choices and have opportunities to participate in authentic learning with high-stakes outcomes.

THE PROCESS

As collaborators, we were keenly aware that we had to step out of the way more than usual to allow students to mature as independent thinkers and critics. In short, we had to share authority for teaching and learning with our students. At the same time, we were strangely excited about the possibilities that emerged as we designed the process for the year-long project. Starting with the seed idea of providing an environment where students had an opportunity, in front of peers, teachers, and outside judges, to defend a work as great, we understood that the outcome had to truly matter to the students. That meant we needed to fully embrace being a guide, so that it was not our voice alone steering the force of the classroom.

Instead, we had to trust in the students' curiosity, encourage them to poke at canonical texts (novels and stories and poems deemed sacred by critics and scholars), allow them to change their minds, and let go of "getting through the curriculum." And there was a lot we had to let go of. From controlling the texts students chose (what if a sophomore chose *Harry Potter*?), to being sure that students were really reading (as if we ever know that anyway), to designing a common assessment that demonstrated that all students had learned the same concepts (even though we philosophically believe in knowing and inspiring the uniqueness of each child). So, we began with the end in mind. Students would, before a panel of judges, defend a work of literature as great, and, as our pièce de résistance, the winning book would be added to our curriculum the next year...even if it were *Harry Potter*.

Given the stakes of the outcome and the skill sets expected of our students, we dedicated three-quarters of the year to instruction, practice, and research. This process went as follows:

- Discuss and debate the concept of greatness (not limited to literature).
- Apply refined definitions of greatness to each text we read ranging from a contemporary graphic memoir to a canonical Shakespeare play (thus practicing the art of argumentation and public speaking).
- Review teacher criteria for the project (each personal text had to meet a minimum of two prerequisites to be eligible).
- Submit choices to teacher for approval.
- Begin independent reading and research while simultaneously reading and critiquing texts in the curriculum.

The last four weeks of the year were then devoted to preparing the defense, which was comprised of three parts:

- two- to three-page paper arguing book's greatness in three categories.
- tri-fold poster detailing the author's context, the reader's response, and critics' reception.
- two- to three-minute persuasive speech delivered to each student's class (and a panel of English faculty).

Each English class (and selected English faculty judges) voted on the most persuasive speech (in content and delivery), and the winner of each section moved on to the final round, delivered in front of a panel of faculty and administrators.

THE OUTCOME

Because we gave them agency, students bought in to the process, which was a critical component to this project's success. And while some students chose their authors safely (John Green), others went big (Anthony Burgess). All, however, faced the same stakes.

By upping the ante as educators (professionally, philosophically, intellectually), we modeled the value of risk-taking. We walked our students' walk. By taking a back seat, we moved students' critical thinking to the foreground and were rewarded. Ultimately, two different approaches to greatness stole the show, each argued eloquently, intelligently, and convincingly. Marveling at the text he had chosen, one of our winners reflected, "Like other great literature, *The Kite Runner* is a stunning work of art. Hosseini writes with such precision that words seem to fly off the pages." Another curriculum changer spoke of the philosophical challenges his book posed, "Aldous Huxley makes us question our very own happiness in life and whether it is stimulated by cheap and easy means."

By year's end, each student made deliberate choices about literature and learned to evaluate and deliberate with maturity. And, after a lot of hard work, they debuted their critical thinking and orating skills on a public stage, and took a gratifying bow as defenders of greatness, but also as defenders of choice and autonomy in a dynamic classroom they helped to build.

Evan Brooke taught English at St. Andrew's during the writing of this research-informed article.

Susheela Robinson teaches English at St. Andrew's and is the former head of the English department and a CTTL workshop facilitator.

Putting It Together: The Mega-Awesome Research Project

The prospect of a research project does not thrill every student or parent. The work, lost weekends, and extra stress discourage some learners. But that's not why I'd never included one in my class. The reason I'd never asked students to do a research project is because I didn't know how to teach it. Even worse, it seemed boring, and "boring" will doom any project.

I used to deflect questions about its omission and inwardly insisted that my students acquired these skills through other endeavors. Now when someone asks, "Are there any large projects?" I respond, "Well, there's the Mega-Awesome Research Project, but it's just too mega-awesome for me to explain right now!"

When I finally embraced a research project, I enlisted the help of my colleague and the school's librarian, Sarah Stonesifer. We sought an experience that would teach useful skills, allow student choice, encourage cooperative learning, and provide varied opportunities for students to present their findings. Above all, we didn't want "boring"; we wanted to thrill our students with engaging, rewarding (dare I say novel?) work.

What about the research process? How do we, as mindful educators wanting to teach research, evaluation, and analysis skills, manage the information overload that can overwhelm even the savviest of web surfers and attention spans? The process for finding sneakers, a primary source, a homecoming dress, or the perfect scholarly journal article is the same—because no matter what, information-seeking is the central goal. The inquiry process, one that goes beyond just finding the information, is defined by Daniel Callison and Katie Baker as:

1. **Questioning**, realizing that there is a question to be answered and formulating an initial thesis or research question.

2. **Exploring ideas**, learning more about connected concepts, and identifying potential helpful (internet or physical) sources.

3. **Assimilation** begins once potential starting points are identified, becoming immersed in detailed information, re-assessment of prior knowledge, and rejecting of more tangential ideas.

4. **Inference** happens after the majority of data gathering, where the application of acquired knowledge connects with original analysis.

5. **Reflection** is where the researcher adjusts the final output based off evaluation, and reflects on the methods.[177]

Guided by Sarah's vision of the research process, we created a project to match our goals. The project revolves around one year in history, and each student completes a research project on a different historical figure who was alive during the selected year. For six weeks, students work individually and collaboratively to research their figures, connect their lives, and relate them to the key events and historical movements of the year at the center of the project. It's big. It's fun. It's the Mega-Awesome Research Project!

A partial list of the fun components all students complete includes:

- Analyzing cryptic primary sources with a team of investigators seeking to unveil which year lies at the project's heart. (That's right—we make them figure out the year themselves!)

- Crafting newspaper-style obituaries for the historical figures.

- Curating museum exhibits on one aspect of each figure's life and producing a brochure showcasing the artifacts on display.

- Drafting 50-word (no more, no less!) mini-sagas that express one event in each figure's life as a compelling narrative.

---

177 Callison, D. (2015). *The Evolution of Inquiry: Controlled, Guided, Modeled, and Free*. Libraries Unlimited.

- Producing short documentary films on events and historical developments occurring during the relevant year.
- Displaying a massive timeline illustrating each figure's connection to the year.

All the elements of a traditional research paper remain. There's still a thesis argument built on primary sources. Students still find, evaluate, and study sources, constructing appropriate bibliographies as they work. We teach source citation skills and note-taking systems, and how to go from outline to draft to final product. The Mega-Awesome Research Project is better than the traditional research paper because its many elements motivate our eighth graders to showcase their unique abilities.[178]

The volume of work still intimidates some students, but by the project's spring launch, they are ready. We have already taught, modeled, and practiced many important skills, and our approach, with its emphasis on support and process, encourages students to produce their best work. The project continues to evolve, and I look forward to improving it every year. I love my students' surprise and pride at their own hard work and creativity, and the satisfaction we all share upon the project's completion. The project has reinforced my sense that research is a crucially important skill that must be taught. Students can access unfathomable amounts of information; we must not only teach them how to do so well, but make sure that they want to.

Scott Corkran teaches humanities and history at St. Andrew's and is a Middle School Grade Dean. Sarah Stonesifer was the assistant librarian during the writing of this article.

---

178 Barron, K. and Hulleman, C. (2014). *Expectancy-Value-Cost Model of Motivation.* In *International Encyclopedia of Social & Behavioral Sciences* (2nd ed), Oxford University Press.

Knowing vs Knowing About

WHAT DO YOU TEACH AND WHY?

When I made the jump to teaching high school, having emerged from the lucrative fields of being a grad student and then an adjunct professor, I didn't have the smoothest of landings. There were many reasons, I suspect, but one of them was that I thought the stuff I was teaching was so intrinsically cool that all I had to do was share this stuff and all would be hunky dory. As I floundered with bored and cranky students who were not only not inclined to find my stuff cool, but were decidedly disinclined, a young, hot shot history teacher reached out to me.

"I fool kids into thinking that I'm teaching them history," he said, "but in reality, I'm just using history as a means to teach them skills." For a while, I thought my younger colleague was right, so I explicitly altered my approach to focus on skills and attendant neurocognitive constructs—receptive language, visual processing, higher-order cognition, etc. But I have lost faith in that approach. In part because many students aren't any more interested in skills than they are in metacognitive approaches to teaching; instead, what interests them the most is, dare I say, knowledge.

In a sense, I have returned to where I started. Knowledge is not information—that you can get on the internet. Rather, knowledge may include information, as well as skills, but nevertheless goes beyond them; it has the power to inform the way we live, want to live, or ought to live. It is intelligible in general terms and is almost obvious, and yet knowledge reaches its most lively comprehension in specificity.

Knowledge includes that which is usually taught in school, but intuitively involves much more. It generates the love for and from our respective disciplines. There is, after all, a significant difference between knowing and knowing about stuff. Many teachers teach about stuff, but great teachers begin from a position of knowing and orient their students toward it.

DOXASTIC KNOWLEDGE AND OBJECT KNOWLEDGE

To put a more technical spin on it, let me borrow a distinction made by analytical philosophers between "doxastic knowledge" and "object knowledge."[179] Briefly, doxastic knowledge is largely propositional and includes the stuff that is usually taught in school, with its various sub-distinctions. It includes de dicto knowledge, that is, stuff that I can say. For example, "The wall in my bedroom is green." Doxastic knowledge also includes de re knowledge, which is the stuff that is contained within that which is spoken about. Thus, "And I know that the green wall could have been made from a mix of blue and yellow paint." It also includes practical knowledge, including what my young colleague called skills. "I not only know that my wall is green, and what makes green green, but I know how to make green green."

Doxastic knowledge (de dicto, de re, and practical) is absolutely essential for sound pedagogy, but it falls short of what is, or ought to be, the goal of great education: object knowledge. Object knowledge (knowing) is more inspiring, lively, and productive than doxastic knowledge (know about/knowing how). Object knowledge is qualitatively different in that it intuitively teaches us what we should teach, why we should teach it, and how. It is both the beginning and goal of teaching and thus ought to inform how we approach our discipline.

A STORY ...

Suzie is an intrepid and curious student who is intrinsically motivated and endowed with all the skills that we would want in a great student.

---

179 My discussion of doxastic and object knowledge relies heavily on Nicholas Wolterstorff, "Knowing God Liturgically," *Journal of Analytical Theology*, Vol 4, May 2016.

She also has a mom—Suzie's not a robot. One day, Suzie decides that she's really going to get to know her mom, so she brings all the attributes of being a great student to bear on getting to know her mother. She conducts primary-source research using sound methods; she contextualizes her research using only peer-reviewed publications, locating her subject in its proper milieu; she carefully deconstructs her sources, both primary and secondary, to expose their biases and the unconscious roles that they play in supporting dominant power structures; she sprinkles her prose with nifty terms like "othering," "binary," and "intersectionality." She attends mother-daughter social activities and workshops to hone her interpersonal communication skills. Suzie's interest, grit, and productivity ultimately earn her a PhD from a prestigious university. She concludes that her mother, though given to the contingencies of her times and thus having flaws, is a thoughtful and loving person. In the introduction to her dissertation, Suzie says that she feels she knows her mother better than she knows her own self—she may even, because of the scope and depth of her research, know her mother better than her mother knows herself. She announces, in the final sentence of the introduction, that she's proud to call her subject "my mom."

Suzie really knows her subject; doxastically speaking, she's a bona fide expert.

But Suzie has never actually met her mom. She was never held in her mother's arms after a fall on the playground. Suzie was never praised after bringing home an outstanding report card. She never rolled her eyes after being disciplined for talking back. She never had to "deal" with her mom after they both had a long day. . . Suzie knows about her mom and has the skills to learn even more, but she doesn't know her.

And then one day, Suzie meets her mother. And their relationship, typical ups-and-downs aside, flourishes. Suzie is delighted, mildly so, that her research was more-or-less spot on. But she knows (and we all know) that her doxastic knowledge about her loving mother, though interesting and insightful, is qualitatively different than the object knowledge that comes from actually knowing, loving, and being loved by her mother. The object knowledge she acquired after meeting her mother includes, but goes far beyond, the doxastic knowledge she had before.

FROM WHERE AND TO WHAT

What Suzie's story suggests is that teachers should orient their students, even if it's beyond the reach of a classroom, toward the object knowledge of their respective disciplines. This is what makes for the most lively and inspiring forms of education. While quasi-controlled experimental data may or may not support this assertion, anecdotally it seems that this is exactly what makes my colleagues—especially that young hot shot history teacher—so good at their jobs. Intuitively, they begin from and push toward object knowledge. The great physics teacher down the hallway loves physics, and that passion drives him to develop pedagogical means capable of manifesting this love. The inspiring English teacher at the other end of the hall loves poetry not only because of the play of language, but also because it sheds light on persistent aspects of life. The superb history teacher stirs students with demanding and passionate arguments, compelling students to respond with care and rigor. My colleagues strive to be better teachers for the sake of their students, but they also do so for the love of their disciplines.[180] They don't merely want to teach, I suspect; they want to teach the stuff that they know and love.

So, object knowledge is the starting point of great teaching, and it is also the goal. If it is object knowledge of the physical universe that inspires the physics teacher, then it is sharing that knowledge that inspires his students and awakens in them a sense of wonder and joy at the complex beauty of the world around them. In many cases, it is the taste of that knowledge that draws them to learn more.

Imagine Suzie, having enjoyed the object knowledge of what it was actually like to be loved by her mother, deciding that she preferred the old way—that the safe and controlled confines of doxastic knowledge were enough. That's possible to imagine, I assume, but it also seems highly unlikely and, frankly, foolish. It would be akin to a great English teacher saying, "Eh, I've read enough." Doesn't happen. Just as the pleasure of reading inspires the English teacher to read more, so the joy of knowing her mother inspires Suzie to get to know her mother better. And that is

---

180 See: West, M. (2017). "Literary Desire", *First Things* (27 July), https://www.firstthings.com/web-exclusives/2017/07/literary-desire.

what students really want. They want to be inspired to know the cool stuff that inspires their teachers.

The Need for Humility

Object knowledge engenders a kind of intellectual humility. To really get to know her mom, Suzie must not know everything about her. She must actually possess intellectual humility to gain further object knowledge of her mother. Suzie must be patient and allow knowledge acquisition to happen as the relationship unfolds, with all the requisite twists and turns of any durable relationship. In the end, it is her mother, in the context of their relationship, who must teach Suzie who she is, and this learning will continue indefinitely. In similar fashion, a good history teacher who knows her stuff, endeavors to let the past speak to the present in as honest a way as possible, avoiding the pitfalls of presentism. History teaches the history teacher and her students, not the other way around.

WHAT AND WHY?

So, what do we teach and why? Great teachers teach object knowledge, as a beginning and end, with the stuff of doxastic knowledge along the way. Why they do, I suspect, is in large part because it tells them, and by extension their students, something about what they love. There is a subjective element there, but there is also something object or external at play. Studying what and how we can better know what we love suggests something intrinsically valuable, worthwhile, and pleasurable about the world and our place in it.[181] Why we teach, or why we want our students to learn what we teach, is that they might too experience, however inchoately, the stuff that has drawn us outside of ourselves and kindled the intellectual humility that makes us want to learn more.

Troy Dahlke teaches religion and philosophy at St. Andrew's.

---

181 Ibid.

Afterword: Our Challenge for You

In the book *Neuroteach: Brain Science and the Future of Education*, Glenn and Ian concluded with a "10% Challenge": "How can you use research-informed practices from the field of mind, brain, and education to transform 10% of how you teach and how your students learn?" The challenge, often perceived as "doable" has been well-received and often met. So we thought we would create a new challenge for readers of this book.

Over the years, we have taken individual copies of *Think Differently and Deeply* to each of the workshops we have conducted, whether it is at conferences such as researchED, SXSWedu, Learning Forward, or Learning and the Brain, or work with individual public and private schools or districts. As part of those sessions, we have teachers select an article or two of their choice to read and then discuss with a reading buddy. We do this to provide examples of what research-informed teaching and learning can look like and how doable such evidence-informed teaching and learning design is even in the lives of busy teachers. The feedback we often get is how nice it was to actually sit quietly, read, and then discuss an article during a professional learning experience.

When we conclude our version of "drop everything and read" we ask the question, "What would it take for your school, district, or program to create your own version of *Think Differently and Deeply*?" That question is our challenge for you. Dr. David Daniel often talks about creating a science of teaching field research-base that should come from the teacher and an evidence-generating protocol that should focus on: What is the problem, need, challenge, question, or opportunity, what research strategy or promising MBE principle might work for an individual student, group of students, or whole class, and did it work in your context with your students? Sharing these in a narrated form, such as the articles presented in this book, creates an accessible and teacher-friendly way to build the science of teaching research base.

So our challenge for you after reading this book is to create your version of *Think Differently and Deeply* and to share it with educators—in print or virtually—around the world. This way, a science of teaching and learning field will evolve by those on the front lines of changing the brains and transforming the academic, social, emotional and identity development of each individual student.